WARRIORS WITH WINGS

THE BOBBS-MERRILL COMPANY, INC.

A Subsidiary of Howard W. Sams & Co., Inc.

Publishers • Indianapolis • Kansas City • New York

WARRIORS WITH WINGS

The Story of the Lafayette Escadrille

BY EDWARD JABLONSKI

illustrated with photographs

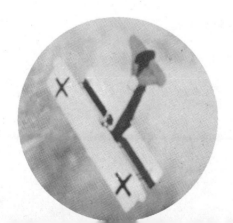

For

PREFACE

Although a half century has passed since the Lafayette Escadrille first flew into action, the story of the men who formed it and their selfless principles, courage and dedication remains timely. There is always need for men who are capable of seeing ahead, valorous and devoted to a cause. Of course, following the terrible waste of life, the hypocrisies, the blunderings and betrayals of trust of the First World War, causes, altruism and even patriotism became almost passé.

Still, this did not affect the motivations of the men who gave or were willing to give their lives because they believed that civilization itself was facing extinction.

If the men of the Lafayette Escadrille were the first Americans to become air fighters, they were also the first imbued with that broader patriotism: a devotion to all of humanity. However much their efforts were exploited by their leaders and their sacrifices denied by postwar "peacemakers" (who were really out for revenge and plunder), what this unique band of Americans accomplished can never be cheapened. What they gave was honestly and freely given.

Their "work," as they called it, was as dangerous as it was romantic and there can be no denying that many chose it because of the adventure, glory, danger and exhilaration in knowing that they were doing something that no men had ever done before them. In this sense they were pioneers; that the science of aviation advanced tremendously during 1914–1918 is now a matter of history.

It is also historical fact that aviation played a small role in the outcome of the First World War. Neither aircraft nor the strategy of its use in war was developed highly during a war commanded primarily by men whose military thinking remained safely on the ground and deep in the nineteenth century. The Second World War would prove the early pioneers correct in their belief in the impact of air power. This near-orphan, this military misfit, would from 1939 to 1945 demonstrate what a terrible weapon had been forged in the skies over France two decades earlier.

Aside from their contribution to the advance of aviation, the development of what would become known as air power, the men of the Lafayette Escadrille, most of them at least, would demonstrate the meaning of American character. They were an attractive band. Not even Hollywood could have gathered together such a cast of characters—and their adventures defy fiction.

Only thirty-eight Americans served with the unit known as the Lafayette Escadrille, which in time grew into the larger Lafayette Flying Corps. This is the story of the original escadrille, not of the entire corps. There is an important distinction between the two because many after the war who had in fact been with the Corps claimed to have served in the Lafayette Escadrille. Fine men served in the corps, but the original escadrille was, and still is, proud of its uniqueness.

Acknowledgments

I am indebted to Rear Admiral Edwin C. Parsons and Colonel Carl H. Dolan, two ex-Lafayette Escadrille members, for all their help and encouragement on this book. Admiral Parsons, who is president and historian of the Lafayette Escadrille N. 124 Society, very generously offered to read the manuscript to check for accuracy. His comments were flattering and valuable. Admiral Parsons' own book, *I Flew with the Lafayette Escadrille* (originally entitled *The Great Adventure*), happily back in print, is certainly one of the truest and most delightful ever written about experiences in aviation during the First World War.

A special debt is owed to Colonel Paul A. Rockwell of Asheville, North Carolina, for his kind interest in this book from its very beginning. Throughout its writing he has been cooperative, freely giving of his time and wide knowledge of the history of the Lafayette Escadrille. Colonel Rockwell with characteristic generosity granted full permission to quote from his own books and from letters of his brother Kiffin. He also placed his full collection of Lafayette Escadrille photographs, most of which he took himself, at my disposal. It would be impossible to thank Colonel Rockwell enough for his full contribution to this book.

Further thanks are due to Colonel G. B. Jarrett for pictures from his collection; to Colonel C. V. Glines, Chief, Magazine and Book Branch, Office of the Assistant Secretary of Defense, for his assistance; to Royal D. Frey of the Air Force Museum, Wright-Patterson Air Force Base, Ohio; and to Robert McGrath, World War I Aero Book Shop, West Roxbury, Massachusetts. A special thanks is owed to my editor, Betsy Harvey, who was forced to contend with a very messy manuscript laden with odd spellings, wayward construction and semantic curiosities.

E. J.

I do not consider that I am fighting for France alone,
but for the cause of humanity,
the most noble of all causes.

KIFFIN ROCKWELL

1 YOUNG EAGLES

The five graceful, almost dainty, deadly little Nieuport fighter planes strained like zealous insects intent upon springing into the sparkling morning air.

Their rotary engines, cylinders spinning around inside the motor cowlings, clattered and roared, then wheezed but did not die out. All five aircraft, whose engines combined to make a shattering racket on the peaceful French meadow, were freshly painted. Some were a soft cream color all over, others were splotched light and dark shades of brown. On the underside of both top and bottom wings were painted red, white and blue circles, indicating that the planes belonged to the French *Service Aéronautique*. Broad red, white and blue stripes were painted on the rudders. They were colorful fighting machines.

The slender wings vibrated and fluttered with near-human impatience and excitement. The clumsy wheels (which underneath their canvas covers resembled bicycle wheels, spokes and all) nudged against the wooden wheel chocks. The motors barked and thundered; the bracing wires hummed in another, higher key. The smell of gasoline and castor oil was in the air. The racket, the tension, expectancy, the very smell of the factory-fresh Nieuports were exhilarating to the pilots waiting in the cockpits.

A most curious fact about the event was that four of the five pilots were not French but American.

It was barely dawn: May 13, 1916. The United States had not yet been drawn into the Great War—the war that would later be called the First World War. It would in fact be a year before the United States declared war on Germany. But these four adventurous Americans, and others like them, for reasons of their own could not wait. They watched impatiently for the signal to take off from the tiny airdrome at Luxeuil in southern France. Almost a hundred miles due east was the trench line of the Western Front, like a slender scar across the face of France from the sea in the north to the border of neutral Switzerland in the south.

The Great War, in its second year, had settled down to a deadly stalemate in the trenches. Great battles were fought, men died by the thousands every day, but to little advantage. Nothing was resolved and the conflicts resulted only in the publication of long casualty lists. Modern war had taken the warriors unaware. Using the latest weapons—the machine gun, gas, the tank and the little-understood airplane—the old generals soon found that the old theories of war did not mean very much. Confused, though

The Fokker E-III, the Eindekker, *the first warplane on which a machine gun was mounted to fire through the propeller arc. Synchronized to fire only when the propeller was not in the line of fire, the front-firing machine gun gave the Fokker pilots a great advantage over Allied pilots. Note also the rotary engine, which whirled around as fast as the propeller.*

too arrogant to admit it, they engaged in pointless battles and succeeded only in killing appalling numbers of men.

Flying in 1916 was a risky and daring adventure in itself, not to mention engaging in snarling dogfights ten thousand feet above the trenches. Before the airplane was recognized as an important weapon it was regarded as a kind of toy, the plaything of foolish, wealthy sportsmen who placed small value on their lives. But during the first few months of the war it had developed into the newest and deadliest weapon and its pilots the most glamorous fighting men since the knights of the Middle Ages.

Their heroism began with the act of getting the planes into the air. The pilots did not consider themselves heroic because of this. They sincerely believed that they were flying in man's most modern invention (the airplane in 1916 was only thirteen years old), the very finest, most highly developed precision machine in existence.

The boxy little Nieuport 11 was the best fighting plane on the Western Front in the spring of 1916. As a fighter craft it was actually better than the German Fokker E–III which about this time had gained so formidable a reputation on the Front. Designer Anthony Fokker had devised for the E–III a method of mounting a machine gun on top of the plane's body and, by using a series of gadgets and gears, enabling the pilot to fire directly through the propeller blades. He merely had to aim his plane at the enemy and fire, an arrangement that assured much more accuracy than did guns mounted on top of wings, fired by a gunner from a cockpit.

Except for the forward-firing gun, however, there was nothing exceptional about the Fokker E–III. It was difficult to control and maneuver; it was flimsily constructed and sometimes fell apart in the air and—if the synchronizing gear between gun and propeller was not working properly, if the timing was slightly off —a pilot could shoot off his own propeller in an air battle. Nor was the Fokker very speedy—at its very best it could barely go ninety miles an hour. (The *E* in its designation stood for *Eindekker,* meaning single-wing.)

The Nieuport, which the pilots affectionately called *Bébé,* was a biplane. The upper wing measured less than twenty-five feet; from tip of propeller to tip of tail the *Bébé* did not cover twenty feet. This little killer could fit in a fairly large living room; a half-dozen might roost on the wing of a modern Boeing 707 jet airliner.

Bolted atop its upper wing was a single .30-caliber Lewis machine gun. It was up there so that it could be fired over the arc of the revolving propeller. The pilot fired the gun by pulling a cable which dangled into his cockpit. Fastened to the gun was a circular metal drum which held only forty-seven rounds of am-

An air battle over the Western Front; such encounters were called dogfights by Allied pilots. Note: This may not be an authentic photo but does capture the feel of air fighting very well.

Cockburn-Lange Photo: G. B. Jarrett Collection

munition, a supply it did not take long to use up in an aerial free-for-all (pilots called them "dogfights"). In this case the pilot had to change drums in midair and, as often as not, in midcombat.

The pilot would then have to stand up in the cockpit, pivot the gun (with the barrel pointing up at a nearly ninety-degree angle), remove the empty drum and replace it with a full one. All this time, while standing in the blast of air from the propeller—one hand on the stick, the other on the drum—the pilot had to worry about the enemy taking shots at him.

There were other hazards. The joke was that the *Bébé* (or any other model of Nieuport) had two speeds: *On* and *Off*. Once the motor coughed into life, the plane was ready to leap into the air like a nervous dragonfly, unless restained by the ground crew, who held the wings or put wooden chocks under the wheels. There was a good deal of wild force in the front of the aircraft since the engine revolved as fast as the propeller, a blur of whirling metal. In the air it required much alertness and skill to keep the plane under control. If the pilot did not fly the plane literally every minute, his own aircraft could prove as ruthless and fatal as any enemy Fokker. Nor could the pilot dive at too steep an angle or for very long. That could shred the fabric off the wing, or worse: the wing itself would collapse or blow off into the propeller slipstream. There were no parachutes in 1916, at least not in tiny fighter aircraft.

Whatever the many dangers, even before they encountered an enemy plane, the four young Americans seated in the Nieuports would not have traded places with anyone. They had already seen the war on the ground, as infantrymen in the French Foreign Legion or as volunteer drivers in the American Ambulance Field Service.

But it had not been like this on the ground. They knew they were about to embark upon a great adventure—they would make history. Not only were they to fight for a cause in which they believed—protecting France from the invading Germans—they were the first Americans ever to fight in the air. Further, they were the first all-American fighting squadron, the *Escadrille Américaine* or, more officially, N. (for Nieuport) 124.

After what seemed to them like hours of warming up, the four Americans finally saw Captain Georges Thénault, assigned by the French high command to lead the American squadron, hold up his arm and then drop it. The signal to take off!

En l'air!

The ground-crew men let go of the wings and pulled the chocks from under the wheels. The planes shuddered; the din was ear-shattering as Captain Thénault turned into the wind and bounced his Nieuport along the field. On one of the bounces he managed to keep the *Bébé* in the air. The propeller knifed into the morning mist, blowing back wispy swirls as the little plane nosed upward toward the Vosges Mountains to the east. It was just a few minutes after six o'clock and the sun's rays flashed over the white peaks.

The other snarling, sputtering machines followed the Captain with nervous eagerness. Kiffin Rockwell raced ahead, followed closely by James McConnell, Victor Chapman and William Thaw. They climbed to join the Captain circling over the field, then took their positions for their first patrol—or *sortie*, as it was called.

Thénault had carefully drawn a diagram which looked like a flattened V, indicating the position of each plane on the patrol. Because he and Thaw were the most experienced pilots, they were to take the rear positions above the other three planes. Their job would be to keep a lookout for German planes above, hiding in the sun (which were always difficult to see). It was a favorite tactic to dive out of a cloud above a formation, through a formation, shooting all the while and keep going to avoid further combat. Surprise attacks were always the most costly—and Thénault could not take any chances on the first patrol.

"Remember," he cautioned more than once, "this is a routine sortie. We will fly the course as planned. No one is to seek out combat. We must maintain formation."

The Captain noted that although the pilots nodded in agreement, mysterious smiles and flashing glances were exchanged.

Thénault stood in his handsome blue uniform of the French Flying Service. He was nearly six feet tall and the perfect picture of an officer. To suggest that he was older than his twenty-nine years, he had grown a neat little mustache. Deep-set eyes revealed a sensitive and kindly temperament. He was a favorite of his "young eagles," as he called the Americans. But he also realized that he would face problems in discipline, for they were a headstrong crew, particularly Kiffin and Victor.

In the air, he would see how they performed.

The formation, with Kiffin leading, was climbing up to 7000 feet in the direction of Germany. At this altitude they began to run into misty clouds.

McConnell, who had never flown in the area before and was afraid he would lose sight of his companions, tried to climb over the clouds in order to see better. He was quickly enveloped in the mist and could see neither Rockwell nor Chapman.

Flying behind the trio, Captain Thénault was studying the formation flying of his little band. It was not neat.

And now where was Mac?

Having emerged from the thin cloud layer, Thénault could see Kiffin's and Victor's planes, but where was Mac? Anxiously the Captain searched the skies for a stray Nieuport.

"To the south I made out the Alps," McConnell later reported. "Their glittering peaks projected up through the white sea about me like majestic icebergs. Not a single plane was visible anywhere, and I was growing very uncertain of my position."

Then the Captain saw Mac, apparently disoriented by his flight through the cloud.

Eh bien! There was Mac, in the brand-new Nieuport flying toward Switzerland! Should he come down in neutral territory, it would cause an international incident of great complexity. A supposedly neutral American would be interned by neutral Switzerland while flying a French plane. Besides losing the pilot, France would also lose a factory-fresh Nieuport. It would be a most unfortunate beginning for the all-American squadron.

Signaling as best he could to Thaw to keep an eye on Kiffin and Victor, who were still on course for Mulhouse across the lines, Thénault dived toward Mac.

Mac himself had begun to worry—"my splendid isolation had become oppressive"—and began twisting his neck about looking for the others. He spied Thénault's plane coming for him and watched with some interest as the Captain waggled the wings, dipped the plane and waved his arms in desperation. Mac waved back.

The Captain seemed excited and waved more strenuously. He pointed to the north until Mac saw the other three planes. Mac banked the *Bébé*, nudged the rudder and joined the Captain. In a few minutes they were back in their loose formation and practically over the lines.

There was No Man's Land, pockmarked with shellholes and indented with irregular lines which appeared to have been made by an insane worm: the trenches. The Nieuports were up nearly 10,000 feet and the pilots could not make out the finer details— the shattered trees, the mud, the burst of artillery shells. Even the sound of the big guns was muffled by their engines.

But Thaw, Rockwell and Chapman could well remember how it had been down there with the infantry. All three were veterans of trench service with the French Foreign Legion. The air service was gloriously different: no barbed wire, no muddy trenches, no bayonet charges, no rats, no bombardment——

Suddenly in their midst there was a blast of black oily smoke; an orange-red center flashed briefly. The Nieuports rocked from the concussion. There was another blast, and another. Soon there were blotches of smoke on all sides of them.

They were definitely over the lines and the German antiaircraft guns had gotten their range. Even so, the bursts were exploding all around them without doing any actual damage, a situation that gave Kiffin Rockwell the opportunity for a little sport. Leading Mac and Victor, he dived into the black splotches in an aerial game of tag. The three enjoyed skylarking for a few moments and then continued on their sortie.

They were now up well over 10,000 feet and a wide stretch of the earth lay below them. They could see the Rhine River, a narrow silver meandering line, the Black Forest and several German cities.

At that altitude it was freezing cold even in their fur-lined flying suits. McConnell noted that he was forced to breathe deeply because the high air contained less oxygen.

Soon they were over an area in which there was supposed to be a German airfield, but no enemy planes rose to challenge the patrol. There was some disappointment in that, for Mac, Kiffin and Victor were eager for their first encounter with the enemy. Thaw had already had some encounters and could wait. Captain Thénault was happy to be spared further incident.

All planes returned to Luxeuil in good formation after the two-hour patrol—or, more accurately, when their fuel was low and they had to land.

They were greeted noisily by the other Americans, Norman Prince, Bert Hall and Elliot Cowdin, who had had to remain on the ground because there had not been enough planes to go around. Most of the war materials at that time were being shipped to the Verdun sector, more than 250 miles to the north, where a great battle raged. Prince had not helped matters just a few days before the squadron received its first planes. On a practice flight he had managed to fly a Nieuport borrowed from another squadron through the wall of a hangar. He had all but demolished the plane and damaged the hangar, but he had emerged from the crackup without injury to anything but his reputation as a pilot.

As he watched the men talking excitedly, gesturing and whooping, Thénault joined his second-in-command, Lieutenant Alfred de Laage de Meux, who had also remained on the ground.

"And how did it go?" he asked, grinning at the Americans walking away from their planes.

The Captain's eyes sparkled. He smiled and said, "They will do, Alfred. They will do, indeed."

2 ESCADRILLE AMÉRICAINE

How had these nine oddly assorted men come together to fly in battle over the tortured fields of France? And why did seven of them, not Frenchmen at all, wish to give their lives if necessary in a war that was none of their business? Who had brought them all together?

Although many were responsible for the organization of the all-American squadron and the initial idea to form such a unit may have occurred to several people, Norman Prince had furnished the enterprise with his own energy and persistence.

It was not a simple matter to convince the French to form a squadron of American volunteers in the early months of the war. But Norman Prince did not easily take *no* for an answer, nor did he give up because of the seemingly endless and time-consuming obstacles.

The eager volunteers who flocked to the French colors, as well as those who hoped to enlist in the British forces, were faced with a serious decision: to take the oath of allegiance required on enlistment. It meant that the Americans were renouncing their American citizenship—something they did not wish to do, no matter how devoted they were to the cause of France and England.

There was a French loophole, however, furnished by the famous (and at times infamous) French Foreign Legion. The refuge of the world's adventurers, misfits and fugitives was the Foreign Legion. Though part of the French Army, it required no formal oath beyond a promise to obey orders. If the young men from good homes and genteel backgrounds did not mind rough and raffish company, the Legion was the place for them to fight "for the cause of humanity."

A strong, unselfish, almost spiritual belief in this cause was the driving force of most volunteers who fought in the First World War before the United States became a belligerent. To some perhaps it was an outlet for adventurous spirits. These men had no real conception of what war was about or what they were letting themselves in for. But to most who served in the American squadron, fighting for France was a crusade in the name of civilization and culture. Their reaction to the declaration of war by Germany on France in August 1914 was immediate and uncomplicated by doubt. On August third, for example, the day of the declaration, Kiffin and Paul Rockwell, two brothers from Asheville, North Carolina, had already offered their services to France. Four days later they were on a ship headed for war.

Among the first who wished to offer their services was Norman Prince. As a boy he had spent a great deal of time in France, where his family had a summer home. Later, as a young man, Norman hunted in the Pyrenees Mountains near Pau. He loved the French countryside just as he admired the French people, whose language he spoke fluently.

Norman was the younger of two sons of Frederick and Abigail Prince. He was born at Prides Crossing, Massachusetts, on August 31, 1887. The Princes were a distinguished New England family; Norman's grandfather had once been mayor of Boston. His father had, however, made his mark—and wealth—in the world of business. The two boys, Norman and Fred Junior, grew up in a pleasantly comfortable atmosphere, wanting nothing. Their way of life endowed them with a sense of security, a fine education as well as that poise and attitude which is the mark of what was once called an aristocrat. On the other hand, it may also produce an individual of independent thought, stubbornness and explosive temper. These qualities may not have made Norman popular at all times, nor made for good relations with his father (who had a similar temperament), but it made him the ideal man to push through his idea for an American squadron.

Norman revealed an early adventurous streak. As his father once noted, "he began hunting when he was seven and he never showed a sign of fear." Both Norman and Fred were devoted horsemen, often taking part in the hunts that were held regularly at Prides Crossing. On one of those days their father had decided, because of a steady downpour of rain, that the boys should not ride.

As usual the boys took the decision manfully, but the pleading glint in Norman's eyes affected his father.

"The turf will be too slippery and riding will be dangerous," he told them, feeling that a little explanation was due.

Norman's eyes glistened.

"Yes, sir," he said to his father. Then he and Fred exchanged glances, looked down at the floor and sighed audibly.

"We had hoped so much to ride today," Fred managed to say as he looked through the tall window at the steady rain. "It's really not a very bad day, sir."

"I think it's beginning to clear a bit—there," Norman added, pointing toward the gray east.

Frederick Prince suppressed a smile and appeared to be lost in deep thought. Both boys were excellent riders. Perhaps he was being too protective. You do not produce men, he thought, by sheltering boys. Of course their mother would be most unhappy if they went out on such a day. The rain was bad enough, but to ride in it was worse.

"You would be careful," their father said, "if I gave you permission to ride, wouldn't you?"

Norman and Fred all but swore a deep oath in an attempt to assure their father of their good intentions. He smiled again, secretly proud of their spirit and self-confidence.

Whooping, the boys ran to the stable, mounted and rode off into the drenching rain.

During the hunt neither Norman nor Fred betrayed his father's trust. They rode carefully and took no chances, but after the hunt was over and it was time to return home they decided to have a little sport.

"Race you to the stable!"

The horses were off and running. In the excitement both Fred and Norman paid little attention to safety precautions. Each was intent upon arriving at the stable first.

On one of the turns they were racing neck and neck. First one would surge ahead, then the other; then at top speed the two horses came together. Thrown off balance, the animals slipped and skidded in the wet earth and both Norman and Fred were thrown in a tangle of arms and legs.

Then all was quiet in the meadow except for the sound of the rain. A groan signaled that Fred, with a broken collarbone, had regained consciousness. He lay painfully without moving, wondering what had happened to Norman. Then he heard his younger brother's shaking voice; it was edged with pain but was not without a touch of Norman's usual humor.

"Fred," Norman croaked, "I think I'm dead. How do you feel?"

Norman's broken thigh and Fred's collarbone fracture ended their riding for a few weeks. But, once healed, they were back at it as enthusiastically as ever. If one is to enjoy life to the fullest, they believed, he must also be willing to run the risks.

Norman grew into a sturdy young man. Not tall, he seemed even shorter because of his broad shoulders and athletic physique. He had sandy hair and his aristocratic good looks were partially hidden by a scraggly sandy mustache. With his bright smile, bustling manner and penetrating blue eyes, Norman's personality could best be described as forceful and sunny.

For all his sense of fun, his daring and gallantry, Norman was able to concentrate his energies on things other than riding and hunting. On completing his education at Groton he went on to Harvard, from which he was graduated with honors. He completed his education at the Harvard Law School in 1911. After passing the bar examination, Norman Prince, now twenty-two, chose to pursue a law career in Chicago.

Prides Crossing was a good distance from Chicago—undoubtedly one of the reasons that Norman had selected that city. He and his father had already had some major disagreements, one of them over Norman's interest in flying. In 1911 Norman had enrolled under an assumed name in a flying school and had earned his pilot's license. The following year he sponsored the design and construction of a racing plane. This craft was to fly in the already world-famous Gordon Bennett Trophy Race, which took place in Chicago that year. Unfortunately the Burgess Racer, as the plane was called, was not completed in time for the competition, which was won by a sleek Deperdussin monoplane from France.

Norman's devotion to aviation was no playboy's whim. During this period, naturally enough, most aviators were rich young men or free-lancing adventurers who flew around the country giving exhibition flights at fairs and circuses. While Norman was not above enjoying the thrills and risks that came with flying, his interest in aviation was serious and scientific. Had not war intervened he might have become famous as one of the early pioneers of aviation.

So it was that when the war erupted in Europe that fateful August of 1914, Attorney Norman Prince's mind was preoccupied with flying. Shocked by the ruthless invasion of Belgium and then France by the seemingly invincible Germans, Norman decided to do something about it immediately. Hoping to serve with the French as an aviator, he enrolled in the Burgess Flying School at Marblehead, Massachusetts, to brush up on his flying.

At the school Norman met Frazier Curtis, another flying enthusiast also dedicated to the idea of fighting against the German invaders. Already past his midthirties, Frazier was a bit old for air fighting, but it was his dream to serve with the British Royal Flying Corps. Unlike Norman, Curtis was unable to speak French.

At this time young men from all over the United States were trying to get to France. But it was probably at Marblehead that the idea of making up a fighting unit of American aviators to fight for France was conceived.

Like those other young Americans, Norman and Frazier strongly believed that the cause of France and England would one day be America's cause. But an even greater number of Americans maintained that a war in Europe belonged in Europe and that there was no point in America's interfering. In addition, many Americans sympathized with the Germans. Time, of course, as well as a number of tragic German actions, would prove Norman correct. In the meantime, the President of the United States, Woodrow Wilson, announced that his country would "maintain a strict and impartial neutrality."

There were some stormy sessions between Norman and his

father about Norman's decision to fight in France. Prince Senior exploded when Norman told him.

"To France?" he shouted. "Don't you realize there is fighting going on there, and killing?"

"Yes, sir," Norman answered as calmly as he could. The Germans were, by the end of 1914, within sight of Paris—they could see the tip of the Eiffel Tower. The great battle that would be known as the First Marne had been fought; the Germans had been stopped, but at great cost. France, Norman's "second country," was in deep distress. Everyone had heard stories of the German atrocities in Belgium. Surely this was humanity's war, not a mere international squabble.

"What of your law practice?" his father demanded. "Can you afford to neglect that for a few months while you carry on with your foolish crusade?"

"That will take care of itself until I return," Norman answered.

"And what if you do not return—have you considered that?"

"Yes, I have," Norman replied. "But I feel I must go. If the Germans win, there will be no future for any of us."

"Nonsense!" his father exploded again, his face reddening. "The French and the Germans have been at it like this for centuries. Let them keep their little wars."

"But this is not a little war," Norman protested. "Already it involves France, Germany, Great Britain, Austria, Russia, Belgium—even Japan. People are already calling it a world war, the Great War."

"And now you want to make it Norman Prince's war?"

"It will be our war in time, I am certain," Norman said, ignoring the sarcasm.

"We have a great ocean to keep us out of your Great War," his father retorted.

"With the airplane that great ocean will not mean much."

"Those sputtering kites!" his father answered. "You crazy

birdmen are lucky indeed if you can keep them up long enough to get them across a drainage ditch. The airplane—good Lord!"

Norman was ready to give up; there was no point in going on. Neither of them would give in. He stood up.

"I am sailing for France on January twentieth, sir."

Frederick Prince stood up as if he had sat upon something sharp. The color drained from his face. He spoke quietly.

"So you have made up your mind," he almost whispered.

"Yes, sir—and I hope to serve in the French Aviation. Good-bye, sir."

He turned and made for the door.

"Norman!"

"Yes, sir?"

"Good luck, Norman—and God bless you."

Norman came back into the room and took his father's hand. His grip was powerful. "Thank you, Father."

Aboard the *Rochambeau* a few days later Norman met other young Americans on their way to France. He did little other than talk about his idea of an all-American volunteer flying unit. The young men, many on their way over to enlist in the Foreign Legion or to offer their services in the American Ambulance Field Service as noncombatants, were intrigued by the idea. Some, naturally enough, preferred to take their chances in the trenches. That was risk enough without fighting in a flimsy plane.

Among those who listened avidly to Norman's plans was a youth from Ossining, New York, with the impressive name of Edmond Charles Clinton Genêt. He was twenty but appeared at least five years younger, with a baby face, round and pink, and blue eyes. Young Edmond had an even deeper tie with France than did Norman; he was the great-great-grandson of the some-what infamous Citizen Genêt, French Minister to the United States during the presidency of George Washington. (Genêt's activities in the United States, his attempts to raise troops to attack Spanish Florida and to commission American ships to prey on British commerce led to his recall. Instead of returning to France, where he was supposed to have been guillotined, the earlier Edmond Charles Genêt remained in America. He eventually married the daughter of George Clinton, the first governor of New York and later a Vice-President of the United States.)

Genêt, who was deeply religious and much aware of his ties with France, sailed on the *Rochambeau* with the words of Thomas Jefferson etched in his mind. At the time of Citizen Genêt's visit Jefferson had said that the cause of France was "the most sacred cause that ever man was engaged in." Jefferson was referring to the French Revolution, but Edmond, Norman and the others found it equally true in 1915.

The boy with a baby face was on board the *Rochambeau* quite precariously: in order to obtain a passport and to enlist in the French Foreign Legion he had lied to the French consul about his age. Another reason also tended to make him shy and not given to talking about himself or his background: Edmond Genêt was a deserter from the United States Navy.

Their ship docked late in January, after which the young Americans dispersed. Norman and Edmond said goodbye. Though both were to serve in the American escadrille, they would never meet again.

Norman made his base a hotel in Paris. From this luxurious headquarters he proposed to lay siege to the French High Command with his idea for an all-American squadron. He was soon joined by Frazier Curtis, who had not been successful in enlisting in the British air service because of the stumblingblock of the oath of allegiance. Discouraged, he decided to join Norman in Paris and see if he could get into French aviation.

Soon another possible recruit joined their ranks: Elliot Cowdin. A New Yorker, son of a wealthy manufacturer, Elliot was like Norman a Harvard graduate. When he met Norman and Frazier he was already enlisted in the American Ambulance Field Service. Norman's enthusiasm for aviation and the promise of aerial adventure soon convinced Elliot he too should become an American flyer.

But convincing the French there should be an American squadron was another proposition. With his perfect French, his self-assurance, poise and affability, Norman had little trouble getting in to see "the right people" at the Ministre de la Guerre. The various officials he met and spoke with greeted him warmly, agreed with him in his views on the cause of France, smiled back at him—and did nothing. The French had their hands full —the war was not going well for them and there was no time to think about new problems; the old ones were bothersome enough. Besides, there was no shortage of dashing young Frenchmen eager to serve in *l'Aviation*. Too, there was the question of American neutrality and all the international implications that brought into the picture.

There was one other item: the French had had one unfortunate experience with an American volunteer, a young man by the name of F. C. Hild. In the early confused weeks of the war Hild had offered himself as an aviator, learned to fly at the expense of France—and then deserted. He returned to the United States, where he proceeded to criticize the French and France. These remarks were picked up by the newspapers and certainly gave "aid and comfort" to the Germans. It was even hinted that Hild had sold military information to the Germans. So far as the French were concerned there might be another Hild among these eager Americans.

So the French High Command let Norman Prince's idea become buried under a pile of official paper. Anyone with less dedication and resolution than Norman would have given up in the face of official disinterest. Just the job of filling out the endless forms would have been discouraging enough.

All through the frustrating weeks Norman lost neither his determination nor his warm smile—nor did he ever show fatigue. In one thing he succeeded: five weeks after he arrived in France, on March 4, 1915, he enlisted in the French Air Service. By talking fast and pulling strings Norman was able to join up without going through the formality of enlisting in the Foreign Legion. So that he would not forfeit his American citizenship

Norman merely promised to obey orders, as did the Legionnaires. Because of his previous flying experience he was given preferential treatment.

Norman was sent to Pau for military flight training; his station was not far from the fields and hills where he had spent so many happy days in peacetime France. He was to become a bomber pilot and would fly the Voisin, a great clumsy two-seater. He was not happy with this prospect, for he wished to fly alone in an *appareil de chasse* (pursuit plane, fighter), although he was delighted to see Elliot Cowdin, also a student bomber pilot, at Pau.

At least they were in it, Norman felt. That was a good step. But to his father he wrote, shortly after reporting at Pau, "Some day soon we will all be united in one escadrille—an *Escadrille Américaine*—that is my fondest ambition. I am devoting all my spare energies to organizing it and all the American pilots here are giving me every encouragement. . . ."

Besides Norman and Elliot Cowdin there were two other Americans at Pau at the time, James Bach and Bert Hall, both of whom had already served in the Foreign Legion. They liked the idea of the American escadrille very much and hoped to become members of Norman's dream squadron. James Bach would never realize this wish, for after completing his training he took part in many spy-dropping missions. He would fly spies and saboteurs over the lines into German territory and often fly back and pick them up. This was hazardous work, for if the pilot was captured he would be tried and shot as a spy. The Germans detested *franc-tireurs* (or soldiers of fortune), and they regarded any American serving with the French as such.

As fate would have it, Jimmy Bach made history—but never, as he would have wished, as a member of the *Escadrille Américaine*. He was the first American in the First World War to bring down a German plane. Later, on the morning of September 23, 1915, Jimmy volunteered, with another pilot, to fly two spies over the lines. They managed to land, but the second pilot cracked up on takeoff. Looking back, Jimmy, who had made it from the rough field, returned to pick up the hapless other pilot. On his second takeoff, the propeller of Jimmy's plane shattered against a tree stump and it was only a matter of time before the two men were taken prisoner. Thus did Jimmy Bach have another "first" to his credit: he was the first American to be taken prisoner in the war. He eluded execution only because he was able to afford a clever German lawyer for his trial. The Germans were suspicious of the two pilots and their two planes, each of which could carry two passengers—especially when a railroad was blown up in the near vicinity. Though he was not executed, Jimmy Bach languished for thirty-five months in German prisoner-of-war camps.

Bert Hall, the other ex-Legionnaire at Pau, was a more mysterious character. He rarely told the same tale twice, although he talked a lot. He boasted about being able to fly, and then when he attempted his first flight he flew his training plane through a hangar. He said he was a Kentuckian, unless he happened to say he was a Missourian. There was little his friends or the authorities could find out about him. When war came he had been driving a taxi in Paris and was one of the first to report to the Legion office for enlistment. He was a strange man and the French, after their experience with Hild, were determined to keep their eyes on him.

Frazier Curtis, Norman's longtime aide and companion in the crusade for the American squadron, was, like Jimmy Bach, fated not to become a member. He tried hard, but it soon became obvious that he would not make an aviator. After three successive accidents he was sent on sick leave to recuperate and, in time, was released from the French Air Service. He continued to help Norman in the organization of the American squadron by writing letters and getting in touch with his fellow countrymen serving in the Legion or the Ambulance Service. Those who expressed an interest in flying would be kept in mind if the hoped-for squadron ever materialized.

On one of his recruitment visits to the men in the Ambulance Service, Frazier Curtis heard about a Dr. Gros from many of the drivers. "He's talking about getting up a whole flying corps," Frazier was told. Someone else was apparently thinking along Norman's lines—only more ambitiously. Ordinarily a French *escadrille* consisted of some six pilots. Dr. Gros had plans for a corps, out of which several squadrons could be formed; thus American pilots could be sent to the French squadrons as the need arose. It was not quite what Norman had in mind. Sending the Americans to different French units spoiled his idea for a single American fighting unit.

Dr. Edmond Gros was a successful American physician whose practice in Paris made him well acquainted in Parisian society circles as well as among politicians and the military. A most ambitious man, Dr. Gros, with his neat though drooping mustache, piercing eyes and ramrod bearing, looked more military than medical. When war came he immediately became an important figure in the organization of the American Ambulance Field Service. This unit supplied ambulances, bought with American money, as well as the volunteer Americans to drive the ambulances. For some reason the idea of flying had captured Dr. Gros' imagination, as it had so many others', and he undoubtedly thought of forming his American corps about the same time Norman was dreaming of his escadrille.

The two Americans may have disagreed on the size of the unit, but Norman could not deny that, as Dr. Gros later said, "the war was not a local conflict between European nations, but a worldwide struggle between the forces of Good and Evil."

Using his powerful influence, Dr. Gros made it possible for Norman and Frazier to reach those members of the French military who would be able to help and would also be interested in the idea. As one early sympathizer with Norman had emphasized in a letter to the French Ministry of War, "It appears to me that there might be great advantages in the creation of an American Squadron. The United States would be proud of the fact that certain of her young men, acting as did Lafayette, have come to fight for France and civilization."

The next sentence was even more telling: "The resulting sentiment of enthusiasm could have but one effect: to turn the Americans in the direction of the Allies." In short, the young volunteers would serve as propaganda agents, attracting both American attention and sympathy.

Meanwhile, as Dr. Gros talked, bullied and pulled strings, Norman Prince waited. He had arrived in France in February 1915, and the months drifted away into summer, then autumn. Winter came and he seemed no closer to the realization of his dream than when he had arrived almost a year before.

Norman was not idle, however. On completing his training at Pau he was breveted (officially declared a pilot) and sent to Escadrille V.B. 108, in which he was to pilot the Voisin bomber —a great, curious-looking plane whose wings spanned no less

Voisin bombers, early French planes which the Lafayette men protected from Germ fighter planes. A Bébé Nieuport flies over.

Courtesy Paul A. Rock

...e of the few actual combat photographs of the First World War. A French Voisin has ...t been set in flames by a German two-seater.

than forty-eight feet. It was difficult to maneuver, was slow (top speed barely sixty miles an hour) and because of its inability to climb to high altitudes, it was vulnerable to ground fire.

Piloting a bomber was not so exciting as flying a fighter, but it was no less risky. This was especially true during the early months of the war, when few military men understood anything about the employment of aircraft in combat.

When Norman was sent to the Front, the Germans had only recently introduced their Fokker monoplanes, the *Eindekkers*. Synchronized to fire through the revolving propeller blades, the forward-firing gun proved a deadly innovation. All the pilot had to do was point his plane at the enemy and press the trigger: the airplane had been transformed from a toy into a gun platform.

The Allies, though working on a similar gun, did not yet have one when the Fokker appeared on the Front. The French and British planes were still equipped with guns which fired over the propellers or were manned by a gunner in a second cockpit in the plane. The single machine gun mounted in the front cockpit of the Voisin that Norman flew had a limited range of fire. It could not fire toward the rear at all and only partly on either side of the plane. Enemy planes soon learned to attack from the rear. Before long the planes of the Allies were being described as "Fokker fodder."

During the eight months (from May through December 1915) that Norman Prince served as a bomber pilot, he frequently found himself in a tight spot. This was the result of his plane's lumbering flight characteristics and the advantage the Germans enjoyed with their new Fokkers. After one mission Norman returned to his base with his gunner dead in the front cockpit and the Voisin practically in tatters. Another time he brought back a seriously wounded gunner. But Norman was unscathed—it was as if he were immune to German bullets; it was an immunity that held even to his death.

Like every pilot, Norman longed to give up being a "truck driver," as bomber pilots were termed, and transfer over to the *Aviation de Chasse*. He was by nature a hunter and not a delivery man. Instead of an unwieldy bomber or observation plane, he hoped to fly the graceful, darting Nieuport.

Expectedly the gears began to mesh. Norman, Elliot Cowdin and William Thaw, another American who had been flying for months, were granted leave to go home in December 1915. On their return to France they were to be trained to fly the Nieuports in anticipation of the formation of the American squadron. The personality and power of Dr. Gros were not to be underestimated.

When the three Americans arrived in the United States they were greeted as heroes—and villains. Welcomed in some quarters as knights in the service of civilization, they were cheered and asked to speak on the war in Europe. But there were dissenting voices. Soon there were demands published in German-language papers, as well as in Washington, that the three Americans be interned. They were, technically, French soldiers in a neutral country. They were also violating the President's vow of neutrality.

German Ambassador Johann von Bernstorff lodged a complaint with Secretary of State Robert Lansing. Before any official action could be taken, their leave was up and the Americans, with a little connivance on the part of certain officials, slipped out of the country and returned to France.

While this tempest brewed, the resolute and tireless Dr. Gros continued his own campaign. He talked to both French officers and influential Americans living in France—among them William K. Vanderbilt, from whom Dr. Gros hoped to receive financial assistance for his *Escadrille Américaine*.

Calling upon Mr. and Mrs. Vanderbilt one day, Dr. Gros outlined his idea for an all-American squadron. When Dr. Gros finished speaking, Mrs. Vanderbilt acted with swift resolve.

"She walked to her desk," Dr. Gros later reported, "and wrote out a check for five thousand dollars. . . ."

Fixing her husband with a glance, she said, "Now K, what will you do?"

Vanderbilt, long an advocate of American intervention in the war, added $15,000 to the fund—and a good deal more as time went on. Committees were formed to attend to every possible need of the squadron: the purchase of uniforms, monthly allowances for the men, printing of pamphlets, prize money (for men who were decorated or who shot down enemy aircraft), and various other expenses. The pay of the ordinary French soldier amounted to a sou a day—about one cent in American money. However, in view of his rank of corporal, an aviator earned eight cents a day; American volunteers were granted an additional forty-five cents in the Air Service.

Even in the light of such generosity it was obvious that the Americans could hardly manage on the money they would earn in the French *l'Aviation*. Some, though not all, of the American volunteers (Prince, Thaw and Cowdin, for example) had their own sources of income or could get money from their families. But with the organization of the committee which called itself the Franco-American Flying Corps, thanks to the generosity of William K. Vanderbilt, the money problem was solved.

Norman Prince was happy to learn that his idea, though somewhat touched up by other hands, was finally becoming an actuality. One of the most important reasons was that the French had replaced General Auguste Hirschauer, who had been the Chief of French Military Aviation when Norman first began working on the plan, with the more dynamic Colonel Henri Regnier. Even so, an additional two months slipped by in traditional military fashion before the official orders were published, on March 14, 1916—more than a year after Norman had arrived in France.

On that date the committee of the Franco-American Flying Corps was informed by the French Grand Quartier Général that it had authorized the formation of an all-American squadron, officially designated *N. 124*.

Norman Prince's dream had come true.

3 "... THERE WILL THE EAGLES BE GATHERED ..."

From the lush summer of 1914, when war had erupted, through the spring of 1916, when the *Escadrille Américaine* finally came into existence, much of western France had become a shell-pocked wasteland. Great armies had clashed on this ground, young men died, the armies clashed again and other young men died. Reality had in those twenty months revealed that war was not all romance and adventure. Few families in France were untouched by the war: sons, husbands and fathers were killed or crippled for life; farms lay in ruins; the buildings were flattened and the fields devastated. Even a fresh new spring could not disguise the look and stench of death.

Now when troops marched to the Front the workers in the vineyards seemed not to notice, but continued with their work. In 1914 it had been different—there were bands, people lined the roads where the soldiers marched, and there were cheers. It had been different—indeed, exhilarating. Those who had been there, and still lived, would not forget those first exciting days of the war.

The Paris edition of the New York *Herald* described the departure in 1914 of the first American volunteers for training in the Foreign Legion:

Paris was stirred by their fit and lighthearted appearance as they swung along, the Stars and Stripes and the Tricolor carried side by side, and all along the route from the rue de Valois, where they assembled, to the railway station they had a triumphal passage, cheered on their way by men, women and children, who appreciate their courage and sympathetic co-operation.

They are a particularly fine lot of men, recruited from high and low, all keen and determined, and a credit to France as well as to the country which gave them birth.

Among the first forty-three Americans sworn into the *Légion Étrangère* were four whose lives would become associated with the American squadron: Paul and Kiffin Rockwell, the two brothers from North Carolina; William Thaw, the wealthy young sportsman from Pittsburgh and Weston Bert Hall, the ne'er-do-well from Missouri—or Kentucky. Of the four only Thaw was a qualified aviator at war's outbreak. Bert Hall, however, was claiming this skill and boasted of having already flown two years before in the Balkans. When he was finally sent to a flying school,

Hall's performance was silent proof of his reputation as "the biggest liar in the Legion."

The Rockwells were more typical of the type of young men who rushed to the colors of France in August 1914. Paul was four years older than Kiffin, who was then twenty-two. Both were tall, well over six feet, straight as plumb lines, with long narrow faces, firm jaws and piercing blue eyes.

Paul, who sported the drooping mustache so popular at the time, was the more level-headed of the two. A graduate of Washington and Lee University, he had worked as a reporter for the Atlanta *Constitution* until Kiffin impulsively volunteered their services to France the moment war came. Both brothers, however, shared a deep belief in the cause of France and left for France together on August 7, 1914. There they were caught up in the flurry of color, alarums and excursions and martial music. In December, Paul was the first of the Rockwells to fall. During a patrol between the lines he was severely wounded in the shoulder. After being discharged from the hospital, Paul learned that although the wound had healed he was unable to carry the heavy infantryman's pack. Even though he attempted to rejoin his unit, the French decided to discharge him as unfit for further military duty.

Feeling strongly that his fortunes lay with the fate of France, Paul Rockwell elected to remain there and soon found a place for himself with the Information Section of the French Army. As an official war correspondent Paul Rockwell spent many months at the Front. He was never to be a member of the American squadron, but became its official historian and photographer.

Kiffin Rockwell personified the knightly warrior. He was a believer in good causes, in ideals. His was a romantic but also a strong personality: Kiffin detested sham and any form of dishonesty. His temper was quick and he soon made it clear that any offense to his code of gentlemanly conduct would cause trouble. His mouth tightened and eyes burned as Kiffin let it be known in a soft, almost gentle Southern dialect that he disapproved. Nor did he easily forgive. On the other hand, in the company of companions whose conduct and ideals equaled his, Kiffin Rockwell was a trusted, lifelong and warm-hearted friend.

Like Paul, Kiffin had grown up with the stories of his grandfather, Enoch Shaw Ayres, who had fought with honor on the side of the Confederacy in the Civil War. The stories of such gentlemanly warriors fired Kiffin's vivid imagination. While Paul attended Washington and Lee University, Kiffin was enrolled in the Virginia Military Institute. He revealed an early ambition to follow in his grandfather's military footsteps. However, when he was selected to go to Annapolis, he enrolled instead in Washington and Lee to complete his education.

Kiffin was restless and seemed unable to settle down after graduation. He held jobs in various places from Canada to San Francisco. In time he joined Paul in Atlanta, earning his living in advertising, hoping that time would bring some outlet for his driving energies.

With August 1914, the time had come.

Like all the other eager young idealists, Kiffin was soon to learn that there "is no romance in the infantry. It is only a matter of being a good laborer."

He described some of this side of war to a friend: "Last night I didn't do any guard duty but went about two miles to the rear and brought back a heavy load of stakes for barbed wire. Then I went about three miles along the front to another regiment where we borrowed some barbed wire and brought it back. Then we put it up." In his matter-of-fact narration Kiffin suggested some of the monotony of war. They did most of their work at night, for, as he explained, "We have to be very careful here as the sharpshooters are rather busy and have the advantage of higher ground."

Near Craonelle, the two opposing sides engaged in skirmishes rather than in large-scale fighting. Not far distant from each other, the French kept an eye on the Germans (and vice versa), taking an occasional potshot but not engaging in great battles. At night the Legionnaires would take their posts along the remnants of an old stone wall.

One of Kiffin's friends during this period was a moody young poet from New York named Alan Seeger. This war did not impress the two soldiers as anything more than murder, and the action of the German raiders was to them nothing more than "a desire to kill." It was not a knightly, idealistic war at all. Seeger was to write one of the war's most memorable poems, as well as

In the trenches with the French Foreign Legion, 1914. Kiffin Rockwell in the foreground.
Courtesy Paul Rockwell

a description of his own fate, in "I Have a Rendezvous with Death"—an appointment he would keep in 1916.

Kiffin longed for a cleaner kind of war—if it existed. Tired of digging trenches, carrying wood and wire, and savage pointless little skirmishes, he asked to be transferred to another regiment.

Not long afterward the war of boredom and skirmish was finished for Kiffin. His unit was to take part early in May 1915 in the great Allied offensive which became known as the Second Battle of Artois. After one of the heaviest artillery bombardments, the French launched a powerful and well-prepared attack. It was typically French, typical of their style of fighting during the first year of the war.

The French practiced what was called *élan*—ardor, headlong dash into the battle—or, as one writer put it, "the French people were living in a state of sacrificial enthusiasm for which history shows no parallel."

This enthusiasm took little account of the modern German weapons; the French rather looked down upon the machine gun. And, of course, no real soldier liked to crouch like an animal in the slimy trenches. So the French (and the British, too, for that matter), fighting along classic lines, marched directly into machine-gun fire. Even artillery fire did not always clean out the little nests which held the rapid-firing guns.

Kiffin was yet to learn this new fact of modern war. Here at last was the kind of warfare of which his grandfather had spoken: men fighting and dying like men. When the whistle blew on the morning of the battle he was to exclaim, "I saw the finest sight I have ever seen—men from the *Premier Étrangère* [First Regiment of the Foreign Legion, Kiffin's unit] crawling out of our trenches with their bayonets glittering against the sun, advancing on the Boches."

At first all went well, for the French artillery had stunned the Germans. But then they began to creep out of their dugouts and soon the machine guns stuttered into life. As if some kind of exhilaration had cut off all fear, Kiffin raced along and could see that "as fast as men fell it seemed new men sprang from the ground to take their places.

"To think of the horror of the thing was impossible.

"All I could think of was what a wonderful advance it was and how everyone was going against the stream of lead as if he loved it."

It was unreal. "There is nothing like it; you float across the field, you drop, you rise again. The sack, the three hundred and twenty-five rounds, the gun, have no weight. And a ball in the head and it is all over—no pain."

Kiffin seemed to drift over the chopped-up earth, now littered with the dead and dying. Never had his senses been so alive, never had he been so unafraid. There was shouting—was his voice among those?—and there was the rattle of the German guns coughing and ripping across their front. Then they overran the German trenches. The Germans did not like the bayonets and soon the first line was theirs. A brief rest to catch their breath and they plunged over the top again.

The Germans were on the run, but their machine guns still raked the field like the scythe of death. The deeper Kiffin's unit penetrated into the German lines, the tougher the resistance.

By the afternoon the thrust had been taken out of the Legion's *élan*. Kiffin lay in a hole with an officer and an American named Paul Pavelka, none daring to expose his head because of the withering machine-gun fire. They crouched there for a half-hour listening to the sounds of battle. The firing seemed to have slackened. Had someone taken the German gun?

The French officer popped out of the shelter and, waving his arms, dashed forward, hoping the survivors would follow.

Kiffin jumped up next and, holding his pack before him like a shield, ran after the officer. He ran only a few yards and heard the machine gun crackle on the right. Before he could drop to the ground, he felt a searing rip in his thigh and a shock as if he had been hit by a hammer.

Kiffin was thrown around by the impact and then knocked to

the ground. Pavelka came running up, yanking his first-aid pack from his belt. Kiffin waved him on.

"I'm all right," he shouted. "Go on!"

Pavelka saluted Kiffin with a glance and then was swallowed up in the smoke of the gunfire. Kiffin found he had been struck by a single bullet in the upper right thigh. It was a neat puncture; the bullet had not hit the bone. He bandaged himself and studied his situation.

The fighting had already progressed beyond him; he must get back for first aid. The field of battle came into focus; the pain of what he saw was worse than his wound. The proud men of the First Regiment lay all around him. Had any got through unwounded? Kiffin wondered. Some were dead and lay as if asleep, as peacefully as if they were in their beds. Others had fallen and died in great pain—"no pain," had he said?—and sprawled in grotesque attitudes that mocked life.

Those still alive called for aid, for water; those not quite dead, in terrible agony, begged to be put out of their anguish.

Kiffin closed his ears to their cries as he began crawling back toward the French rear area. Hours later he had made only a half-mile, most painfully. When he met the stretcher-bearers they refused to carry him because there were others more severely wounded. Later Kiffin learned that more than half of the 4000 men in his regiment had been wounded or killed.

With an improvised cane, Kiffin managed to make another couple of miles to a farmhouse where other wounded lay. The next day, his wound throbbing and burning, he hobbled along and hitched rides until he came to an evacuation center. There he was put on a train and put in a hospital in Rennes, not far from Paris.

In six weeks Kiffin was off for Paris, his leg almost miraculously healed, on convalescent leave. He joined his brother Paul, who was active as a war correspondent. It was a warm meeting and the two brothers discussed the war at length; Kiffin no longer believed it would be over by autumn. He enjoyed his leave with Paul; they dined like royalty. This was a great change for Kiffin, who had been living on Legion fare for so long.

On one of these pleasant occasions Kiffin met William Thaw of Pittsburgh. He was dashingly dressed in the uniform of the French Air Service and wore the insignia of pilot on his tunic. Thaw was almost as tall as the Rockwells; his face was broad and round, with a generous walrus mustache on his upper lip.

Bill Thaw was just twenty-one when they met, a powerfully built young man who had begun adventuring quite early in life. The son of a wealthy railroad executive, he had taken an interest in flying while a student at Yale in 1913. Flying was definitely in his blood, and Bill dropped out of school in his second year to devote all his time to aviation. He had learned to fly the Curtiss hydroplane, a primitive seaplane. Soon he was taking up passengers, prominent society people like himself, for pretty high fees. He also made aviation history, although it hardly advanced the cause of flight, when he flew under the bridges that cross New York's East River.

Bill's brother Alexander had developed a special safety device for aircraft, so the two Thaws traveled to France in 1914 hoping to win a prize awarded for such gadgets by the air-minded French. While they were in France war came and everyone's plans were changed.

Bill Thaw immediately presented himself as a possible aviator in the French Army. He met the confusion and indecision so typical of the first days of the war and eventually was refused. He then applied to the Foreign Legion and was accepted. Those were the exciting though hectic days when Americans bluffed their way into the Legion by claiming military service with the Salvation Army or training in an *école militaire* (the French did not have to know that this military school had been attended when the recruit was seven years old).

Like the other American Legionnaires, Bill Thaw experienced

the discomforts, miseries and dangers of infantry life. He suffered through long, painful marches, carrying a hundred-pound pack on his back until his feet were blistered and bloody.

Bill was not a born infantryman; he hated walking and he hated the trench life that came with winter. The war was getting nowhere. One November day Bill stood in a cold trench looking up. Above the infantrymen, in the clean air, were two planes dueling in the sky. They twisted and turned, darting at one another in graceful maneuvers. All along the front, dirty, unshaven, freezing foot soldiers looked up to watch the aerial drama.

Bill Thaw decided in that instant that he would attempt to get into the air service again. During his next rest period, taking Bert Hall and Jimmy Bach, also Legionnaires interested in flying, with him, Bill walked through the snow to the nearest airdrome.

Stationed at this field was an old friend, Felix Brocard, now an officer in the French Air Service. Brocard was familiar with Bill Thaw's prewar reputation as an aviator and, after listening, promised to see what he could do to get Bill, as well as Bert Hall and Jimmy Bach, out of the Foreign Legion and into aviation.

Felix was a man of his word, although ironically the two non-flyers, Bach and Hall, were transferred within weeks, leaving Thaw still in the trenches. He walked again, this time a distance of nearly twenty miles, to see Brocard, who commanded his own squadron at the time and was a respected airman (later he would command an entire group—four squadrons—of France's most famous fighting aviators).

Brocard listened again to Bill Thaw's arguments, and within a few weeks had him transferred to his own Escadrille D. 6. The D indicated that the unit flew the Deperdussin two-seater monoplanes. Bill would serve as an observer and machine-gunner. It was not what he wanted, but it was a step in the right direction.

He asked to be sent to a flying school where he might show that he was a pilot, not a passenger. He proved himself immediately by taking up a Caudron G–2—a plane he had never seen before. The G–2 was a big, primitive maze of wires and struts. It rested on a four-wheel landing gear and its twin tails jutted out behind the wings on booms. It was technically a sesquiplane: its upper wing was a good deal larger than the lower wing.

Thaw was soon put to work piloting observer students and shortly after was posted to a combat squadron, Escadrille C. 42, where he distinguished himself on observer missions.

It was during this period that Bill Thaw met Norman Prince and heard about the plans for an American squadron. Although he liked the idea, Bill preferred to remain with the French until plans were more definite. He preferred, too, the action on the Front to waiting while the French made up their mind.

Seeing Bill Thaw in his aviator's uniform in Paris and listening to his aerial adventures gave Kiffin Rockwell, convalescing from his wound, the idea of transferring to the air service also. Before he returned to his regiment at the end of his convalescent leave, Kiffin applied for a transfer.

Another Legionnaire—Victor. Chapman of New York—unknown at the time to Prince, Thaw or Rockwell, was thinking along similar lines.

When war broke out Victor was a student of architecture in Paris. Like Norman Prince he had been reared in the comfort and security of wealth. Yet even as a boy Victor had not been comfortable or secure; he was moody and withdrawn, a little boy with great brown eyes. His father, John Jay Chapman, was an author who had earned a wide reputation for his fiery essays. Victor's mother died when he was six, which caused him to withdraw even deeper into himself. After he watched his younger brother drown before his eyes when he was twelve, Victor was almost inconsolable. He blamed himself for the tragedy, for he had not been able to save his brother—and, worse, should not have left him alone by the fast-running stream.

Victor grew up into a tall, brooding boy. He was remarkable in many ways, sensitive, gifted, fond of the outdoors, artistic— but he did not excel in school.

"Victor never really felt alive," his father wrote of him, "except when he was in danger." He took chances; he climbed to inaccessible places, he scampered over roofs, he dangled from trees. As he grew older, he also risked his own life to save others —a friend from an icy sea, a child who nearly drowned at a picnic. It was as if he were trying to compensate for the loss of a brother.

Victor and his father were almost strangers. Lacking the outward brilliance of the older man, the boy seemed not to belong in his company. When Mr. Chapman remarried, his new wife became a second mother to Victor and gave him the love and understanding with patience that his mercurial father lacked.

Although he grew into a handsome young man with a shock of dark hair which he parted on the side, Victor revealed himself still a little boy when his temper let go.

Victor was an extremely gentle person, despite his temper. He was very fond of his younger stepbrothers who in turn loved him. When Victor came home from Harvard the two boys climbed over him as they wrestled and pummeled him.

He revealed a talent for art, proving himself gifted in watercolor, so his father sent him to France to study. Victor, his father and his stepmother were in France in August 1914. They fled to England to get away from what all believed would be a war zone.

Victor soon made it clear that he was not happy. Then he hinted that he intended to enlist. What followed was a scene similar to that between Norman Prince and his father. The argument waxed warm.

"You are only hoping to embark on what you think is an adventure," the elder Chapman told him. "You merely wish to evade life's more serious duties."

Victor could only answer, "No doubt this must be it." He stalked from the room, his face pale.

Mrs. Chapman spoke as soon as Victor was out of earshot.

"You are wrong, John," she said firmly. "He has submitted through his humility and through his reverence for you."

Her voice broke and she turned away. She knew Victor better

than anyone alive. "But I had rather see him lying on the battle-field than see that look on his face."

Chapman relented. "Within a week," he later wrote of Victor, "he was in France."

He was in the Legion within hours of his arrival. Victor's regiment was an even more motley crew than the one in which the Rockwells, Thaw and Bert Hall served. His first job was digging trenches near Paris. He thrived on this work; it was as if, after twenty-four years, his life had taken on definite purpose. Victor cheerfully attacked all the generally unpopular chores of the common soldier, from digging holes to peeling potatoes.

Often as not there was gathered around the good-natured giant a crowd of his companions and French civilians watching the "millionaire" make the dirt fly. He attacked all jobs, no matter how unpleasant or dirty, with equal zest and geniality. He was even happier when his unit was finally sent to the Front.

Victor was assigned a position on a *miltrailleuse* (machine-gun) squad, which he wanted because he considered it more exciting than being a mere foot soldier. The powerful six-footer was a valued member on this team, particularly when the time came to dig in the weapon and to lift the logs and heavy timbers used to protect the gun position.

Although their sector was a quiet one, much like the one in which Kiffin Rockwell served his early months in the Legion, an occasional skirmish contributed to the excitement. On one of the rare days of action Victor exhibited his mettle in characteristic fashion. The Germans had dug under the French position, mined the area and detonated the explosives. There was a massive upheaval of dirt, barbed wire and debris.

Victor, shaken but unhurt, could see that one of the men had been buried—perhaps alive—in the explosion. He was halfway up the side of the trench when his captain shouted, "Chapman, where are you going?"

"There's a man under the debris," Victor shouted back, still moving.

"You come down from there!"

Victor glared at the Captain.

"Get down, Chapman! If you move into the open you will be chopped to little bits."

"But Captain, a man is buried under that dirt."

"He is lost, Chapman."

"But he can be saved."

The Captain wanted no arguments. "That is all the Germans want—fools to rush out into their gunfire."

Victor turned away and began crawling up the trench side again.

"Chapman!" The Captain had his gun in his hand. "Return to your post."

Victor could see no point in being shot by his own officer, but as he stalked away he made it clear that he did not like this method of warfare at all. His explosive temper was kept in check and, of course, he realized the Captain was right.

He could be stubborn, however. One day he exposed himself for a moment out of the cover of his position and felt a sharp pain in his arm. His arm felt suddenly warm and then his sleeve began to show red. A bullet had passed through his arm.

One of his friends bandaged the arm and Victor went on with his work as if nothing had happened—he didn't even bother to see the medical officer as he should have. The officer came to Victor. He looked at Victor's arm. There was a neat wound, no serious injury and no broken bone. But in the dirty trenches there was always the possibility of infection.

"You will go to the rear," the doctor told Victor.

"Why?"

"For medical attention in a hospital—that's why!"

"But that isn't necessary," Victor said. "My friend can bandage it as well as any nurse. Please, sir, I don't want to play hookey."

The medical officer was amazed. Most men would leap at the chance to get out of the trenches even for a day or two. But not Victor.

His best friend in the Legion was a man named Kohn, a mathematician in civilian life, one of the few Legionnaires with whom Victor had anything in common. They discussed books, art, politics. "His learning is immense," Victor wrote of Kohn to his stepmother. In his letters to her Victor always played down the dangers of trench life, reassuring her and his father.

One day as he and Kohn stood near their gun, a shot rang out and Victor's good friend collapsed to the ground. Picking him up as if he were a child, Victor carried Kohn to the aid station. It was the only time anyone had ever seen the big American with tears in his eyes.

The medical officer took one look at Kohn and shook his head.

"Save him, sir," Victor sobbed.

The doctor could only continue shaking his head.

"Save him," Victor said desperately. "Save him and I'll give you a hundred thousand francs."

The medical officer, more touched than insulted by the distraught Victor, told him as gently and firmly as he could, "Your friend is dead, *mon ami*. Now go."

Victor did not customarily display his wealth. Because he had always had money he took it for granted and used it only to ease trench life; and he shared all he had with his companions. But money could not buy back the life of his friend Kohn. There was a time, nevertheless, when he was able to do some good with it.

One of the members of his machine-gun squad was, curiously enough, a former German who wanted to fight for France. The Legionnaire came to Victor with a problem.

"They want to send me back," he began.

"But why?" Victor asked.

"The medico says I need to drink only milk—it is my stomach —for the next two weeks. Where is one to get milk in the front lines?"

The German shared with Victor the belief that unless he was seriously wounded he should be in the lines, not at some rear-area hospital. Victor stood up and told his friend, "Do not go. Wait here." He then walked off.

About dusk Victor reappeared—leading a cow. He had simply wandered around the back areas until he found a farmer willing to sell a cow. He bought it and the German Legionnaire had his milk. This luxury lasted for only a week—a German shell exploded in their position, killing both Victor's friend and the cow.

But life in the Legion, except for the rare skirmishes or the small tragedies, was dull. Victor did not feel that much was being accomplished. He wanted to do something effective every day, every moment. Sitting in dugouts and trenches was depressing. It was then that Victor heard from William Astor Chanler, his uncle who was active on one of the committees trying to get an American fighting squadron organized. Knowing Victor's love of action, he suggested that Victor write to Norman Prince, who was already in training for the French Air Service.

This impressed Victor as a wonderful idea; once in a while he had seen the planes going over. He had never thought of himself as flying one, but what an idea! He had grown discouraged in the trenches. Looking back upon his service in the Legion he felt he had "thrown away ten months of my life, neither helped the French nor injured the Germans . . . why should I stay here when a Hooligan out of Paris could fill my place to better advantage?

"The 'dreadful' trenches, where we were all winter, could just as well have been inhabited by women and children for all the good the men did."

Victor wrote to Norman Prince, offering himself as a candidate for the American squadron. When no reply came he became even more discouraged. Eventually he heard instead from Elliot Cowdin, who was helping Norman. Victor, still gloomy, sensed that he might not be wanted, that it was "Prince's and Cowdin's show, they got it up." They wouldn't need him. He even thought of getting out of the war completely. Still, it was worth a try to get into aviation.

After weeks Victor was surprised one August day in 1915 (almost a year since he had joined the Legion) to learn that his transfer had come through. He would enter the air service. As he confessed to his stepmother, "I am prepared to leap with joy when my transfer comes."

The eagles were gathering: Norman was already flying, as were Bill Thaw and Elliot Cowdin. Bert Hall was proving to be a good pilot, and Kiffin Rockwell had received his transfer from the Legion.

Their destinies were slowly converging.

4 LEARNING TO IMITATE BIRDS

Many a letter written home by young Americans in France between 1915 and 1917 opened with the matter-of-fact though prideful words, "I am now in a French aviation school and learning how to imitate the birds. The work is tremendously interesting."

It was at the great École Militaire d'Aviation situated about three miles from the village of Avord that Kiffin Rockwell and

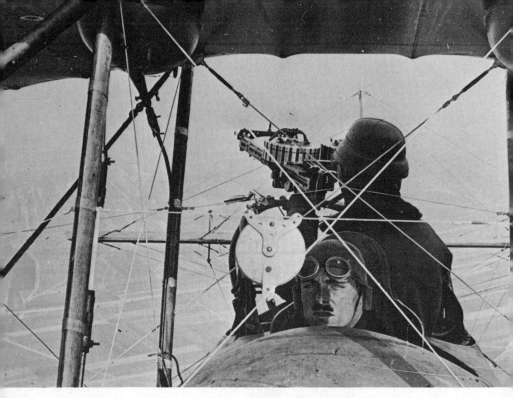

Aloft in a French two-seater. The pilot peers into the camera and the observer–machin *gunner keeps his eyes open for German planes.*

Victor Chapman met for the first time. Both had concluded their service with the infantry and had that in common—though Victor was rather in awe of the fact that Kiffin had been wounded in a bayonet attack. They were now together to learn how to be *pilotes de chasse* and to fly the Nieuport fighter planes of which they had heard so much. Victor had already served about a month with a bomber squadron as a machine-gunner in the Voisin. Also in this squadron were Norman Prince and Elliot Cowdin, hard at work on the organization of the American unit.

Kiffin and Victor became fast friends at Camp d'Avord. Of all the Americans then in France aspiring to action in the air, they were the most similar. They shared a mystical belief in the rightness of the cause—"the greatest struggle between right and wrong in the history of the world," one of their companions phrased it. They felt this even more strongly when on leave in

Paris, or riding in French trains, or just sitting in a café in Avord, when they saw "the women in black." These were the brave widows, almost always with small children, whose husbands had died in the first great battles of the war. Witnessing the cheerful dignity of these women in black made idealists such as Kiffin and Victor feel their efforts were too little.

They shared another quality: absolute fearlessness. They were twentieth-century reincarnations of medieval knights who charged into danger heedless of any risk to themselves. Their cause was just and no sacrifice was too great.

But they were not foolhardy, as was demonstrated during their student days at Avord. They were quick to learn, careful though not overly cautious (which in itself was dangerous) and delighted in flying. It was, however, quite a long time before they were permitted to fly. The French had developed a fine system of teaching student aviators how to imitate birds.

The first bird they mimicked was the penguin. In fact, this primary stage of their schooling was done in planes universally called "Penguins." These were 1909 Bleriot monoplanes, substantially the same plane in which Louis Bleriot had made the historic first flight across the English Channel in July 1909. It was an extremely tricky plane to fly, rather small and light and thus subject to the slightest buffeting of wind or shifting of weight. If the pilot leaned too far, the Bleriot leaned with him.

Its appearance was best described by Edwin C. Parsons, who wrote that the Bleriots "seemed as if they were merely gathered-up odds and ends of wood, discarded matchsticks and the like, which were wired together, catch-as-catch-can fashion, with baling wire to form a fuselage. The old handkerchiefs were sewed together to cover the wings and that part of the fuselage around the pilot's seat. The remainder of the fuselage was left naked, which gave the ship a sort of half-finished appearance." The entire contraption seemed to be mounted on a couple of bicycles. The pilot sat with half his body outside the cockpit, with the propeller whirling just a couple of feet in front of his nose—and the slipstream of this propeller was tremendous. To hold the pilot in, thick leather straps passed around his body.

The Penguins were the standard Bleriot with the wings clipped. They were odd-looking creatures: ungainly moths that fluttered across the field making a terrific racket but never getting off the ground.

"They were possessed of the devil," Edwin Parsons has written, "and showed almost human intelligence in thinking up dirty tricks to play on their unsuspecting passengers. Start two at opposite ends of the field with practically the entire width of the field between them, and somehow or other they'd run together in a horrible collision in the center of the field."

A day's work almost always ended with several wounded Penguins scattered around the field. They were soon wired back into service by the mechanics and the shaken student pilots were given another chance.

The "Boneyard of Pau," after a day's work at the school.
Pieces of old Bleriots litter the hangar.

U. S. Air Force Photo

The idea behind the Penguin was to accustom the student to the movement of the plane on the ground and get him started on learning how to control the flight path of the plane. In those days there were no dual-control planes. The little fighter planes would not hold two men, so the student had to learn by himself, stage by stage.

Kiffin and Victor proved they could make a Penguin cross the field in a straight line without hitting anything or without going into a *chevaux de bois,* or round and round in a circle, like a merry-go-round *(chevaux de bois*—literally wooden horses—is French for "merry-go-round"). This too was a favorite trick of the Bleriot Penguin. Once started on a circular course, it would chase its tail until something snapped, the engine stopped or the plane turned over.

The two Americans were graduated to the next class, in which they were given planes, generally the Bleriot once again, with larger wings and slightly more powerful engines. This gave the *élèves pilotes* (student pilots) the "feel of the air." Not much air —maybe three feet—but to the student it seemed hundreds of yards. Here he learned how to point the nose of the plane up and down as well as to control the plane's side-to-side movement.

Most of the work was done early in the morning and just around dusk. The wind was less apt to blow during those times. The *élèves pilotes* had enough to contend with without being upset by the slightest breeze.

In the air, of course, the Bleriot was a more lethal weapon than on the ground. Keeping it under control took much skill, and even skill was not always enough. The byways around Avord, as well as the other famous French training centers at Buc and Pau, were littered with bent and broken Bleriots. Although many such accidents were amusing, because the green pilots were able to walk away from them to fly another day, some were tragic.

Dennis Dowd was an ex-Legionnaire who had been seriously wounded in the heavy fighting of October 1915 in the Champagne sector. This New Yorker found no romance in war. "I have never seen the kind of bayonet charge I read about," he wrote. "It is usually the slow amble of a lot of brutally tired men, over ground that has been torn to pieces by big guns, so that when the enemy is reached, there is no fancy play with the bayonet as taught at school.

"Men of both sides have a real distaste for that yard of cold steel, and they just poke dully and rather carefully at one another, until one side or the other runs."

Dowd, who had been a successful young attorney, had enlisted in the Foreign Legion for the classic reason: it was said that he had been disappointed in love. He was also disappointed, most tragically, in his wish to serve in aviation with his fellow Americans, several of whom he had known in the Legion.

After recovering from his wounds, Dowd transferred to the flying school at Buc, near Versailles. After passing through all of his preliminary training on the Penguins he had reached the stage at which he was to take his altitude test. For this he was given an old Caudron bomber. He climbed to 3000 feet over the field and then, for no reason apparent from the ground, his plane hung in the air for a moment and then plunged into a *vrille*—a spin.

As the clumsy kite twisted, the men on the field watched with horror. Surely Dennis could pull it out; he was nearly ready for his brevet. Perhaps the months in the trenches, his wounds had weakened him so that when he reached an altitude of 3000 feet (which is not very high) he had fainted. Or perhaps the old bus, which Parsons likened to a flying "chicken coop," just stopped flying. Whatever the reason, the Caudron with Dennis Dowd in the cockpit spun into the ground with a shrieking roar. Bits and pieces of fabric, wood and metal, all engulfed in a cloud of dust, flew in all directions. On August 12, 1916, Dennis Dowd became the first American to die as a student pilot.

The news of this accident, spread throughout the world's newspapers, only served to encourage more enlistments in the aviation service. Though men died by the thousands every day in the trenches, they were only numbers. The spectacular death of an airman, a lone man in man's most modern weapon, was news.

Another Legionnaire fated not to become a member of the American Escadrille was Lawrence Scanlan. In recognition of his shock of scarlet hair he was naturally known as "Red." He was, in the words of Paul Rockwell, "an unusually gallant boy. He was badly wounded in June, 1915, [and] lay for almost three days on the battlefield; he spent a year and a half in military hospitals and, on 1 January 1917, was invalided out of the Legion with one leg six inches shorter than the other.

"He came directly to Paris, and a week later *insisted* his way into French Aviation. His shortened leg was a tremendous handicap. . . ."

The handicap was that it was difficult to manipulate the rudder controls of the plane with his feet. The rudder of a plane, like that of a ship, turns it to the right or left. At high speeds these controls are especially responsive. Turning also required a delicate hand on the "broomstick," the control stick in the cockpit. It was used in banking the plane, or causing the nose of the plane to go up or down.

"Red" lacked that coordination of feet and hands necessary to a pilot. Every now and then "Red" would simply fall out of the sky over Avord. His crashes became legend, but he always seemed to crawl away from them willing to try again. His most spectacular one occurred in the spring of 1917. He had taken off and then, while flying over an artillery school, went into one of his famed dives. His plane dropped through the roof of the school's bakery.

With a great crash, the heavy motor smashed through the tiled roof and crashed to the floor. Only a portion of the rear section of the fuselage and a crinkled wing protruded through the roof.

The cooks had been busy preparing the bread for the next day and the air was filled with debris, cries of alarm and clouds of flour. In the confusion "Red," who for no sensible reason was unhurt, bolted through the nearest window. Miraculously none of the bakers was hurt either, though they scattered in all directions like the flour.

"Red" was limping away brushing the white stuff off when a captain came running up.

"Come on," the Captain shouted, "help me get the dead pilot out of there!"

"I am the dead pilot," Scanlon answered.

Three more, though less spectacular, crashes convinced the French and even the extraordinarily game "Red" Scanlan that he would not make a pilot. He was released, decorated with the *Croix de Guerre* and returned to the United States.

Kiffin Rockwell and Victor Chapman enjoyed comparatively incident-free days as *élèves pilotes*. While they were at Camp d'Avord Bert Hall arrived, having served with a pursuit squadron at the Front; he was in Avord for a rest and to serve as a *moniteur*—an instructor. Victor described him as "a thin-faced, keen-looking fellow." He too was awaiting word on the American Escadrille. Hall was the opposite of the romantic, tall and handsome Victor and Kiffin. He was of about middle height, with a narrow face, and harbored few illusions about the war, "the cause" or patriotism. He was in it for what he could get and looked forward to getting out of the predominantly French outfits and back into the company of his fellow countrymen.

During this same period, the winter of 1915, another American transferred into aviation. He was James McConnell of Carthage, North Carolina. A University of Virginia graduate, McConnell was the only son of a former judge, the president of a small North Carolina railroad. As a boy Jim had spent many happy years in France and spoke the language fluently. When war broke out in Europe, he gave up his job in public relations, as had Kiffin, to serve in the American Ambulance Field Service.

McConnell admitted that at first he was moved by the spirit of adventure—something big was happening in Europe, certainly the biggest thing in his lifetime, and he wanted to have a look at it, to experience it. When the war came, Jim McConnell was, like Norman Prince, twenty-eight years old—a rather advanced age for a real adventurer. Unlike Prince, Mac—as he eventually was called—was a big man, husky, broad-shouldered, with a cheerful smiling face. Good-humored, intelligent and sharply observant, Mac found that a few weeks at the Front with the Ambulance Service began to change him.

Driving an ambulance was more than a routine job, for Mac served with the famous Section 2 of the Field Service, which witnessed the action and heavy casualties during the spring and summer of 1915. When he entered the Ambulance Service Mac had said somewhat defensively, "I'll be of some use, too, not just a sightseer looking on; that wouldn't be fair."

Still, seeing the badly wounded and the dead—some of them his own countrymen—deeply affected Mac. He knew then that he would have to take a more active part in the war. He had heard through Frazier Curtis and others about the efforts to form an American flying unit and, true to his adventurous spirit, Mac asked to be transferred from the Ambulance Service to Aviation. Early in October 1915 he was sent to the school at Pau for pilot training on the Bleriot. This was about the time Kiffin Rockwell and Victor Chapman were going through the same motions at Avord.

Kiffin was the first to be awarded his brevet, making him a full-fledged *pilote* who could wear the red-and-silver wings on his collar. By October 1915 he was flying the Maurice Farman, a big bomber-reconnaissance biplane. For a time he was stationed near Paris in the Paris Air Guard, whose job it was to intercept the German zeppelins which came over to bomb the city. This work was actually quite uneventful, for the wheezy old Farmans had more trouble finding the zeppelins than the zeppelins had finding Paris. Further, the zeppelin bombardment and the French means of fighting back were equally ineffective.

Victor Chapman had trouble learning to fly the fighter planes and was a little longer in earning his brevet; he too was assigned

to Farmans for a time in January 1916, two months after Kiffin
had won his wings. In February James McConnell was ready for
action. Norman Prince and William Thaw were also in training,
learning to fly the little Nieuport after seeing months of action in
bombers.

William Thaw was already a commissioned officer, having
gone from corporal in 1915 to lieutenant in 1916. Although the
youngest of the seven original Americans who made up the
squadron, Bill Thaw proved to be the most mature in many ways
and soon was the unit's strong right arm. It was Bill who first interested Georges Thénault in the project. Thénault was then
commander of Escadrille Caudron 42, in which Bill was serving
as a pilot. The youthful French commander immediately applied
for command of such an outfit if ever it came into being. As his
second-in-command he selected cherubic-faced Alfred de Laage
de Meux. An ex-cavalryman who had been wounded early in the
war, De Laage transferred into aviation when he was released
from the hospital in March 1915.

Both Thénault and De Laage were popular with the Americans, none of whom except Bill Thaw were officers. In the early
months of the war the usual rank of the French aviator was corporal or sergeant. This, however, made little difference in the
American squadron, for all were regarded as equals (which on
occasion made for problems in discipline), and there was an
easy camaraderie. All of them, Thénault, De Laage, Kiffin, Victor, Bill, Bert Hall and Elliot Cowdin, had gained real experience in the air before the squadron was formed. Only Mac had
not had the opportunity to get his combat wings before they
all came together at Luxeuil. Undoubtedly this lack of experience explained why he flew off toward Switzerland on the first,
otherwise fairly uneventful, *sortie*. Not even the antiaircraft
bursts exploding among the planes gave Captain Thénault the
anxious moments the sight of Mac sailing for Switzerland had.
His young eagles would have further surprises for him.

5 FIRST KILL

After seeing the accommodations at Luxeuil for the first time
Mac "began to wonder whether I was a summer resorter or a soldier." He, Victor, Kiffin and Norman arrived on the morning
train from Paris and were met at the station by Captain Thénault
in a staff car.

"I enjoyed the ride," Mac noted. "Lolling back against the
soft leather cushions, I recalled how in my apprenticeship days
at Pau I had to walk six miles for my laundry."

The Escadrille Américaine *(later Lafayette Escadrille) assembles at Luxeuil, May 14, 19*
Left to right: Kiffin Rockwell, Captain Georges Thénault, Norman Prince, Alfred de Laa
de Meux, Elliot Cowdin, Bert Hall, James McConnell and (with hand in pocket) Vict
Chapman.

At the airdrome itself there were even more surprises. They
were met by an army of mechanics, cooks, drivers—more than
seventy men—assigned to looking after the seven members of the
Escadrille Américaine. Mac, Kiffin, Norman and Victor were the
first to arrive. A few days later they were joined by Bill Thaw,
Elliot Cowdin and Bert Hall.

Luxeuil, before the war, had been world-famous for its hot
baths. Now, not far from the Front, it was the site of a military
airfield. The Americans were billeted in a fine villa adjoining the
baths. Meals were served in the dining room of the best hotel in
town. To get to and from the flying field the pilots had staff cars
at their disposal. War had taken a most luxurious turn!

They had everything but planes. While they waited for delivery, they enjoyed drives through the beautiful countryside. But these were more than mere joy rides. The Captain was anxious that all of his eagles be familiar with the area—tall pines, dazzling streams, steep mountainsides—in case of forced landings.

A week went by and the Americans still waited for their promised Nieuports. Finally, during the first week of May 1916 six new, crated Nieuports arrived at Luxeuil. Factory workmen came to assemble them, instruct the mechanics in their maintenance, mount the guns atop the wings and acquaint the pilots with the function of the few cockpit instruments. Three of the planes were powered by 100-horsepower *Le Rhône* engines and the other three by 80-horsepower engines. The most powerful machines Captain Thénault assigned to himself, De Laage and Bill Thaw, the most experienced pilots. The other three were checked out to Kiffin, Victor and Mac.

Still there was no action. The weather was not good after the Nieuports arrived, so flying was minimal. Kiffin took advantage of a break in the weather on May tenth, took off and was enjoying himself aloft when a sudden windstorm blew up.

The tiny plane was tossed around by the storm as Kiffin fought to keep control. With cool skill he pointed the Nieuport into the wind with the engine running on full power. The wind was so strong that the plane remained practically motionless in the air. Kiffin then proceeded, with amazing dexterity and presence of mind, to bring the plane down in the face of the storm. It descended almost vertically, like a toy on a string, onto the field. There the worried mechanics seized the plane and pushed it into a hangar before the wind could do any damage. Kiffin had managed to get it down safely without so much as breaking a wire.

The French had wisely sent the Americans to Luxeuil because it was a quiet sector, at least in the spring of 1916. The main function of their stay there was to give them practice at working as a team. Their first patrol, three days after Kiffin landed in the windstorm, had been a disappointment to the Americans—they hadn't even seen a German plane.

They spent more time talking with reporters and posing for photographs than they did in the air, it seemed. When they saw some of the fake-heroic material some writers had published about them they became suspicious and distrustful of publicity. So far nothing had happened and already they were being described in the papers as knights in armor. It was embarrassing.

To escape such attention and just to be able to enjoy the freedom he experienced in the air, Kiffin Rockwell took off on the morning of May 18, 1916, on a lone patrol. This was hardly in keeping with the French hope that the Americans would learn the importance and technique of team tactics. It was, however, characteristic of Kiffin—and of most of the early war pilots.

He guided the Nieuport up, then flew in almost the same direction the squadron had taken on their first patrol. It was a bright day and he could see for miles in every direction.

He felt fine; the air was sharp and bracing, the sun brilliant, spilling light and shadow over the earth below. Patches of dark and light green intermixed with tan. A silver river curved through the patterns. No Man's Land was the only thing that spoiled the view. It looked as if someone had ruined an interesting picture by erasing part of it and then gouging the canvas.

Kiffin crossed the lines near the German town of Mulhouse. He would patrol for a while inside the German lines just to see what might happen. His lean face felt the sting of the slipstream as he peered over the side of the cockpit for a better view. From time to time he twisted around to study the skies around him. Shading his eyes with his gloved hand, he tried to spot any Fokker that might be hiding in the sun, ready to pounce on a careless lone eagle.

His attention was suddenly brought to his own plane. The engine sputtered, missed, caught again. Then the steady beat of the engine sounded wrong.

What luck! He'd have to turn back. Reluctantly Kiffin gave the Nieuport a little right rudder, banking gently as he turned toward the airdrome. The engine continued to miss. The problem now was, would it hold up long enough to make it back?

Kiffin's sharp blue eyes began searching for a possible emergency landing spot, just in case. He spotted movement about 2000 feet below him, just inside the French lines. Forgetting his engine for the moment, Kiffin concentrated on the movement.

It was a large biplane, almost ghostly white in color, but there was no mistaking the big black crosses on the top wing. It was a German L.V.G. (so-called because it was manufactured by Luft-Verkehrs Gesellschaft). It was obviously on a reconnaissance mission, taking photographs of the French positions. From where he was Kiffin could see its great narrow wing with square tips and the graceful fishlike tail. Most of all he saw the crosses on the wing.

He eased back a little on the engine, pushed his stick forward and dropped down on the L.V.G. About the same moment the men in the German plane obviously spotted Kiffin. The L.V.G. pilot pointed toward Germany and dived for home. In the rear cockpit the observer-gunner trained his gun on the diving Nieuport. He began firing immediately.

With an almost steady stream of lead spouting at him, Kiffin continued with his screaming dive. Unlike the nervous German, he did not pull the trigger release. The German plane grew larger and larger in his sight.

Just above his head he heard a sharp *ping!* One of the German slugs had hit the Nieuport. The Germans were panicky. The enemy pilot turned a white face over his shoulder to stare at the crazy pilot in the Nieuport. Surely they would collide. The gunner continued firing.

Then when he was less than a hundred feet away from the L.V.G.—"just as I was afraid of running into him, I fired four shots, and swerved my machine to the right to avoid having a collision. . . ."

Kiffin pulled up and turned to see what would happen next. The gun in the rear cockpit pointed straight up at nothing. The gunner had fallen back upon the pilot, who had slumped over to the side. Then the German plane turned gently to one side, a little smoke appeared and for just an instant the plane poised in the air.

The nose dropped heavily as the smoke thickened and the big plane fell twisting toward the ground. Following, Kiffin watched with a mingling of triumph and sadness (there were two men in the plane, even if they were "enemy") as the plane fell almost vertically. A big black smudge was all that remained of it in the air. It crashed just behind the German lines and burst into flame.

Kiffin had scored his first aerial victory—the first victory of the *Escadrille Américaine*—the first time he had encountered an enemy plane in the air. Even before he returned to Luxeuil the news had been phoned and thus confirmed (no victory was official unless properly confirmed) by a French observation post near the trenches.

It had not been pure luck. Kiffin's style of air fighting, so typical of him, was also like that employed by the famous English pilot Albert Ball or the French hero Georges Guynemer: the headlong plunge at the enemy, directly into his fire, opening up on him when he loomed large in the gunsights. This took both flying skill and courage—with emphasis on the latter.

Air fighting in 1916 was still mainly a matter of individual combat; the days of formation flying and cool, precise, careful fighting were still in the future. Kiffin and Victor Chapman represented that special breed of pilot who fought without fear for themselves. For them there was "no after the war," as one Ace phrased it.

Kiffin landed, his engine still sputtering erratically, to a great and noisy welcome. He was patted on the back, carried about, congratulated and generally fussed over. Even in the town he was pointed out as the American who had brought down a Boche with only four bullets. Captain Thénault went about smiling.

He had known all along. Kiffin had merely gone out and proved him right.

The next day Thénault gathered the pilots into the meeting room. He was still beaming, it seemed.

"Gentlemen," he told them, "I have an announcement."

The Americans waited.

"We are leaving this sector . . ."

There was some twisting around in chairs, questioning looks. Someone asked, "Where shall we go to, Captain?"

"*Verdun!*"

There was a great shout. Verdun! The greatest battle in history was taking place at Verdun. Since February 1916 the Germans had tried to take the great complex of forts around Verdun. But the French would not let them have Verdun, a name that stirred the world with its overtones of heroism, sacrifice and the power of human will.

At last they would see some real action.

6 VERDUN

"This flying is much too romantic to be real modern war with all its horrors," Victor Chapman informed his father shortly after N.124 had settled at the great field at Behonne, about twenty-five miles behind the Front. As at Luxeuil, they lived grandly in a fine villa, dining well and driving to the field in staff cars.

The *Escadrille Américaine* was nevertheless in the real business of war when they settled at Behonne. It was one of several squadrons which formed Groupe de Combat 12. Additional Nieuports arrived and all seven Americans took part in regularly assigned patrols. While they continued to enjoy comparative luxury and unusual independence, as James McConnell observed, "Our really serious work had begun, however, and we knew it." (Even from the air Verdun, that long-fought-over area, appeared like the lifeless landscape of the moon: ". . . one wasted surface of brown powdered earth, where hills, valleys, forests and villages all merged in phantoms," Victor described it.) The earth seemed to seethe, sending up dirty clouds of pulverized earth as bright flashes sparkled here and there. These were the heavy guns sending more steel and fire into the wasted earth.

The German High Command planned its assault on Verdun as a blood-letting strategy. No Frenchman would permit a German to pass while he still lived. And so as the fortresses around Verdun became a symbol of France's will to resist, so also was its Army ground up as in some giant senseless machine. But the Germans, too, were dying. The two great armies grappled long after each had forgotten what it was supposed to accomplish. It became important only to go on, stubbornly, senselessly and fatally. The Battle of Verdun flickered out during the winter of 1916 at a cost of 750,000 casualties; neither side had gained any ground, neither could claim victory.

When the battle opened the Germans concentrated almost two hundred planes in the Verdun sector in what they hopefully called an "aerial barrage." Planes with black crosses on the wings flew over the battleground almost constantly, spotting for artillery fire, observing the movements of troops and supplies over the one road leading into Verdun. Early in the year the Germans brought their finest airman, Oswald Boelcke, to Verdun.

This young German aviator was one of the first to understand the airplane as a military weapon. A mild and likable man on the ground, he was a ruthless fighter in the air. He also thought theoretically about air power. Boelcke was not so interested in building up his "kill" score as he was in teaching the younger

German pilots how to survive. As an air fighter Boelcke was as calculating and scientific as Kiffin Rockwell and Victor Chapman were heedless and improvisational.

Boelcke was a firm believer in formation flying, so that all could share the risks and protect one another. With Boelcke on the Verdun front in the new Fokker monoplane with the forward-firing gun, the French found themselves in serious difficulty.

One of the first countermoves made by the French concentrated as many of their planes as possible in the area. Among the units sent to Verdun was the famous *Cigognes*, "Storks," so called because each squadron in this unit had painted a stork on the side of its plane. France's most celebrated airmen served in this unit, among them Georges Guynemer, who was shot down over Verdun. After a long convalescence, the slender young French Ace joined forces with the *Escadrille Américaine* in later battles.

Verdun, they soon learned, was the place for action. During the afternoon patrol two days after they had flown into the sector Bert Hall chalked up the squadron's second victory. He, Bill Thaw, Norman Prince and Kiffin Rockwell took off in their Nieuports and headed for Verdun. They were on high patrol, about 12,000 feet, when they approached the area.

Suddenly Bert lost sight of the other three Nieuports, which flew into some clouds. Almost at the same instant he saw below him a German Aviatik, a two-seat observation plane. For some reason there were no Fokkers about—so far as he could see, at least—protecting the Aviatik. Bert pushed the stick, kicked the rudder and swooped down on the German plane.

Unlike Kiffin, Bert did not follow a near-collision course. He tried to find a blind spot underneath the tail. There the gunner in the rear seat could not hit him and he could pour machine-gun fire into the enemy plane. The two planes, twisting and turning, fenced with each other as they lost altitude while the German plane attempted to head for its own lines. The German gunner was, Hall reported, "an excellent marksman." Just as Bert maneu-

A Fokker E-III diving for the attack from behind. The pilot under attack is unable to fire to the rear to counter the assault.

vered the Nieuport into position for a good shot, the German pilot would turn the Aviatik, giving his gunner a good bead on the American.

Bert suffered an anxious moment when a series of thudding perforations stitched along his fuselage, beginning at the tail and stopping about a foot from the cockpit. Quickly he pulled out of the way, skidded on a fast turn and turned back toward the Aviatik. He saw bits of fabric snapping away from his right upper wing. He pulled away again, hoping for another chance at the German. They were down to about a thousand feet over the blasted ground of Verdun.

For an instant the Aviatik seemed to hang in space. Perhaps the pilot had stalled it, or perhaps the wind caught it. Bert saw his chance, pulled the trigger release and peppered the German plane from the engine straight back along the fuselage. He dived underneath and from under the tail gave the Aviatik two more long bursts.

The fight was over. The German pilot and observer were dead and their plane disintegrated in the air during its descent. The wings were torn off in the dive and the fuselage crashed into the French front-line trenches. Bert returned to the field, where he joined in a celebration. Kiffin, Bill and Norman had also returned, unaware of the fight which had occurred so near them. All were elated by Bert's confirmation. It boded well for the future history of the squadron.

A taste of the future came even sooner than they had expected. The next day, May 24, 1916, was packed with action.

Kiffin and Bill had the dawn patrol. They were awakened at three in the morning, had their breakfast and were driven to the field. By daylight they were high over Verdun, just over the German lines. In the early-morning light they spotted a couple of enemy aircraft, an Aviatik observation plane and one of the formidable Fokker monoplanes. Kiffin and Bill exchanged signals, each choosing a plane to attack, and dropped down on the unsuspecting Germans.

Bill had selected the Fokker, which went down after a single burst from his Lewis gun. The Aviatik streaked for home after eluding Kiffin's attack. The two Americans then turned for Behonne to report the victory. Bill was pleased but not terribly happy. "The poor Boche didn't even see me," he commented.

They had returned just in time to have their tanks refilled with fuel to join in the morning patrol. Captain Thénault was to lead. Scheduled to go with him were De Laage and Victor Chapman. Bill was anxious to add another victory to the squadron score, and Kiffin was ever ready to take to the air. All five Nieuports took off and flew in V formation in a northeasterly direction toward the battleground.

The sun was brilliant and the sky was crystal-blue. Thénault glanced back over his shoulder to study, with pride, the nearly perfect formation. The eagles were learning nicely. Before they took off Thénault had as usual cautioned them not to go off on their own private wars. They were to watch him for any signal to attack.

Thénault turned back and saw a massive formation of two-seater German observation planes. The planes were far below them and deep inside the German lines just over Etain. Thénault dismissed the German planes. They were too far away and there were at least a dozen of them. Besides, they were on their own side of the lines.

He was suddenly startled when a diving Nieuport passed under him headed directly for the German formation. Someone plunged at the enemy. Another Nieuport followed, then another. The beautiful formation was a shambles; there was nothing to do but follow. Livid with anger, his heart tight with fear for his inexperienced pilots, Thénault dived in to help if he could. But he knew it was an invitation to destruction.

The surprise attack by the first Nieuport broke up the neat German formation. A few of the big two-seaters immediately streaked for home, but enough remained to form a defensive circle (thus could each plane cover the tail of the other) and fight back.

Victor found himself the target of crisscrossing machine-gun fire. The bullets came uncomfortably close. They spattered through the plane, the gracefully curving tracers, which ignited and could thus be seen as an aid to aiming, concentrating toward the cockpit. His arm burned painfully as bullets cut through the sleeve and sliced into it. Eyes brimming with tears of pain, Victor turned away from the battle and dived for home.

Kiffin arrived at the scene of the battle in time to have several guns converge upon him. Before his eyes his windshield flew apart. Bits of glass and steel ripped into his face, and blood covered his goggles. He could scarcely see. His face searing with pain, Kiffin dived away from the circle of German planes, dropped low and returned to the field.

Soon Captain Thénault and Lieutenant De Laage also landed. Thénault had tried to wave the Americans away from the suicidal fight. They had been fortunate that the customary Fokkers were not hiding in the sun. Even so, Victor's arm was a painful mess and Kiffin's face even worse. But they were lucky to be alive.

But where was Bill Thaw?

Worried, Thénault dashed to the phone and began inquiring.

There was no word. Meanwhile, Kiffin and Victor had their wounds taken care of and were ready for duty again.

Late in the afternoon the phone rang and Thénault heard about Bill: he was in a French hospital. He had fared as had Victor and Kiffin. He had flown into an aerial porcupine, his plane had been riddled and he had been struck in the arm. His elbow was fractured, his left arm became numb, useless and bled profusely. In blinding pain, Bill pulled away from the battle and swung toward the French lines. He was in such pain and bleeding so badly that he was afraid he would faint in the air and crash.

As soon as he was certain he was over friendly territory, Bill sought a place to land. He brought the Nieuport in for a bumpy landing just behind the lines near Fort Tavennes—already so weakened he could not get out of the cockpit. French soldiers pulled him out of the blood-spattered plane and rushed him, barely conscious, off to the nearest aid station.

Once Bill's wounds had been attended to, he hoped to rejoin the squadron. He had suffered a good deal from shock and loss of blood. Imbued with the same spirit as the other warriors, Bill gave the hospital staff an uncomfortable time, insisting that he be released, even sneaking off to rejoin his friends (he even flew his plane with one arm in a cast). He seemed totally unaware of the seriousness of his wound even after he was sent to an American hospital not far from Paris.

Still, as he lay on the cot he could reflect on the strange turns of fortune. The day which began so favorably with the shooting down of the Fokker ended as a fiasco for practically the entire squadron.

In the bustle and disorder almost no one noticed the arrival of a new man. He was a short, swarthy, broad-shouldered pilot who spoke fluent French, colorful though accented English. His name was Raoul Lufbery. Except for appearing unusually incommunicative, there seemed nothing distinctive about Lufbery.

And there seemed nothing significant in his arrival, or the arrival in fairly rapid succession of other Americans. There was Clyde Balsley, a tall, slender, eager Texan who had served with the Ambulance Service; he was followed by Charles Chouteau Johnson, from Missouri and the Ambulance Service; New Yorker Laurence Rumsey had also been an ambulance driver. Dudley Hill, from Peekskill, New York, had a similar background. Finally there was Didier Masson of Los Angeles, who had been a flyer since 1909 but who had served in the French infantry. Although an American citizen Masson had been born in France—as had the mysterious Raoul Lufbery.

With the arrival of the new men, the *Escadrille Américaine* roster had almost doubled. Counting Thénault and De Laage, they now numbered fifteen. The French High Command had decided to counter the heavy German numbers by enlarging its escadrilles. The fighting had become desperate, deadly and massive.

Rarely did a patrol not meet a German plane. Bad weather, forbidding clouds and drenching rain kept them on the ground, however. Endless card games, reading the same old papers and magazines became boring. Worse, the Captain sat for hours practicing at the piano. "It is disintegrating to mind and body," wrote Victor Chapman, "—this continued *inertia*."

He was happy to be able to join the Captain, De Laage and young Balsley on a morning patrol a couple of days later. They were assigned to patrol above the Meuse River, which wriggled down just east of Verdun.

"We stay together, gentlemen," Thénault told them as before. "We will not let any Germans cross the river to interfere with the battle. Nor will we look for trouble, *eh?*" He looked straight at Victor, who smiled and nodded. The Captain then turned to Balsley.

"You will stay in formation," he said, "and do not attack unless I give the sign." Balsley nodded eagerly and hurried to his Nieuport, on the side of which he had had a Lone Star painted.

The little fighters assembled, and crossed over the lines and were turning for patrol. It happened again. This time it was definitely Victor who bolted from the formation.

He had seen a big German bomber on the other side of the river coming toward them. His single impulse was to attack, with De Laage and Balsley following. Before they could even get within range the German bomber had fled. They had nothing to do but rejoin the by-now boiling Captain Thénault and continue the patrol.

Victor was still bored after all the time they had had to spend on the ground. When the fuel supply was low and they turned to go back to the field, Victor waved a merry farewell and landed at a nearby airdrome.

After refueling he climbed up again, hoping to find the bomber. The big plane was nowhere in sight. Suddenly out of this same nowhere he saw five German planes. According to all the rules of common sense and air battle, Victor should have ducked into the nearest cloud and dived for home.

He dived instead at the nearest Fokker. His Lewis gun snapped off a few rounds and suddenly the Fokker vanished. The drumming of machine-gun bullets behind and around him revealed to Victor where the plane had gone. The pilot, obviously an expert, had flipped away, over, and now was on Victor's tail.

The German's twin guns were shredding away bits of fabric as Victor crouched in the cockpit hoping to make his bulk as small as possible. Try as he might he could not shake the Fokker off his tail.

There was a blinding flash, a terrible pain in his head as he was pitched forward in the cockpit. A glassy spider web appeared on his windshield and the Nieuport reeled as Victor involun-

Victor Chapman after his encounter with German fighter planes on June 17, 1916. A finger (at right of photo) points to where a German bullet cut the fuselage of the plane, grazed Chapman's head and went through the windscreen.

Courtesy Paul A. Rockwell

tarily pulled on the control stick. A slug had passed through the fuselage just behind Victor and coursed through his helmet, making a four-inch-long cut in his scalp. Instantly his goggles were covered with blood.

Victor pushed them onto his forehead in order to be able to see and righted the plane. But the German was still there: another stream of bullets sang through the air and clipped a wire, then struck and severed an aileron-control rod just above and to the right of Victor's head.

This last slug threw the plane out of control again. As it spun Victor grabbed the severed rod in his powerful right hand to keep the aileron of the right wing under control. He then eased back on the stick to pull out of the dive.

The German had gone. (Many believed the expert fighter pilot who had dealt so seriously with Victor had been Oswald Boelcke himself. This has never been definitely ascertained. If this was the battle Boelcke described, Victor had been saved because both of Boelcke's guns jammed.)

What Victor accomplished after this near-fatal battle was amazing, yet so like him. With his head wound throbbing, with blood streaming over his face and into his eyes, with one hand manipulating the right aileron and the other the control stick, he actually succeeded in bringing the plane down inside the French lines.

The little Nieuport fluttered to earth, then bounced along on a small field at Froids. When he returned to his own field, Victor, head swathed in bandages, was ready to join the afternoon patrol, which was just preparing to take off.

Captain Thénault was unusually firm this time. He practically ordered Victor to stay behind. But Victor laughed when the Captain suggested that he join Bill Thaw in the hospital. It was an odd scene: a captain and a sergeant arguing like equals. Had Victor been a French sergeant, and had Thénault been a less kindly officer, there would have been no argument. As it was, Victor was one of the most popular men in the squadron. He was considerate, kind and so courageous that all admired and liked him. It was impossible to be angry with him.

The argument ended when Victor remained grounded for the day and the Captain promised him a new and more powerful Nieuport.

Two days later young Balsley got it. He had been on patrol with the Captain, Kiffin and Norman Prince when they ran into at least forty German planes to the north of Verdun. At odds of ten to one there was no point in doing anything but study the armada with awe.

Even as the Nieuports edged around the upper layer, two-seater Aviatik observation planes, the Germans began firing. The Nieuports were too far away to fire with any accuracy. When one of the Germans moved away from the safety of the formation, Norman swooped down to take immediate advantage. He was met by murderous machine-gun fire and one bullet zipped across the top of his helmet, barely missing his head. That was enough for Norman, who kept on going and made for his own field.

Thénault signaled for the rest of his group to turn away from the swarm of German planes and found that only Kiffin followed him. What had happened to Balsley?

The twenty-year-old Texan had, like Norman, found an Aviatik in his sight. He fired a single shot and then his Lewis gun jammed. In an instant he was hemmed in by German planes. He forgot about the stoppage of the gun and frantically tried to get out of the converged fire chopping away at his Nieuport. He sought the safety of a cloud, hoping to dodge the streams of bullets coming from both sides and behind.

"I was then about twelve thousand feet up," he wrote. "It was while I was standing on my head, the belly of my machine skyward, that something struck me. It felt like the kick of a mule. With the sensation of losing a leg, I put my hand down to learn if it was still there."

He had been hit by an explosive bullet which had shattered against a bone in his thigh. From the waist down Balsley's right side had gone completely dead; it didn't feel as if he had a leg there at all. The force of the bullet caused his foot to kick involuntarily, which threw the Nieuport into an inverted spin. By using his hand to push his right leg, Balsley managed to right the plane.

He again heard the sound of machine-gun fire behind him. He dived the plane, hoping to outrun the tenacious German. He was only a few hundred feet over No Man's Land—on the German side; he had to keep up long enough to make the French trenches. He knew, too, that he must not pass out.

He was skimming over the trenches. "I must get home!" ran

through his mind as he tried to keep conscious, control the plane and find a place to land. He spotted a patch of green which to his pain-dulled eyes looked like an airdrome. Balsley kicked the Nieuport to the left and dived toward the ground.

Too late he saw that he had found an isolated green spot between the lines, gnarled over with rusty barbed wire. He had to keep going with his landing. The pockmarked earth came rushing up at him.

His wheels caught in the barbed wire; the Nieuport flipped over on its back, slammed to a crashing halt. Stunned, Balsley, held in the cockpit by the leather seat belt, had but one thought, "I should bleed to death, after all." He was soon jolted out of such dark thoughts when a burst of artillery cracked not many yards away. The Germans were shelling the spot, hoping to destroy the plane and kill the pilot if either had survived the crash. Balsley had felt no pain after the first jolt when the bullet struck. If he were to enjoy a leave in Paris he realized he would need to get out of the plane and away from the middle of No Man's Land.

Unbuckling the belt, he let himself fall to the ground and found he was unable to use his right leg at all. He began crawling in what he hoped was the direction of the French lines. Luckily, the German artillery had stopped firing. Balsley found that he could barely crawl.

Four French *poilus* (infantrymen) had also crawled out toward the plane when the shelling let up. With practiced skill they crept easily under the wire, skirted holes and asked Balsley what was wrong.

"Bullet—in—my—hip," Balsley told them; even the touch of friendly hands caused pain.

"Can you walk?" one asked.

"Mais non," Balsley answered.

When the *poilus* lifted Balsley, "like a beast unleashed, my pain broke from its long stupor." As the four men dragged and pulled him out of No Man's Land, Balsley was near insanity with pain. After what seemed to the wounded man years of torture they reached a first-aid station. Balsley was more seriously injured than even his pain could tell him. The bullet had fractured into several bits which not only broke his pelvic bone and severed the sciatic nerve but pierced his intestines as well. A nearby automobile, which had come by to pick up a balloonist who had jumped when his post was attacked (balloonists were the few airmen of this period who used parachutes), was used to rush Balsley to the hospital at Vadelaincourt, five miles away.

An immediate operation was required, but little hope was held for Balsley. He was in a primitive, overcrowded hospital which, because it was just behind Verdun, was little more than a charnel house. Barely conscious himself, he lay awake in the dismal heat and the frightful stench listening to the groans of the injured and the dying.

One night the Captain was summoned; he rushed over with several of Balsley's companions. The wounded man's temperature had risen dangerously and it was certain he would die. Instead, he lay there on the unsanitary cot—hardly more than a bed of straw—tortured by the ministrations of a well-meaning but incompetent doctor, and lived. A series of operations removed the pellets of exploded shell and, for a year, Balsley had to remain on his back. His real recovery did not begin until he was removed away from Verdun to an American hospital. Eventually he was released from the service, a cripple for life.

Balsley's first visitor at the little hospital at Vadelaincourt was Victor Chapman, who had flown over in his new plane.

"Hello, old boy," he said, looking cheerful and rather odd in his turban bandage. "Here's your toothbrush."

This was typical of Victor. Although shocked at Balsley's appearance and the terrible conditions in the hospital, Victor did not reveal it. He tried to cheer Balsley up and make him comfortable, and he joked about how the wounded man would enjoy Paris in a few weeks.

"Anything I can get you, old man?" Victor inquired.

Weakly Balsley licked his lips.

"They won't let me drink water," he croaked. This was because of the wounds in his stomach, which would have reopened if he drank any quantity of liquid. "All I can do is suck on a wet bandage."

Victor's expressive face clouded. Certainly something could be done. The gentle giant stood beside Balsley's bed. Just then a doctor came near. Victor reached out and touched him gently on the shoulder and asked in French, "Could my friend have oranges?"

The doctor assured him that it would be all right. "But," the doctor asked with a shrug, "where are you to find oranges in the vicinity of Verdun?"

"I will find the oranges," Victor stated and left.

The next day Balsley had one of his severest shocks. The Captain arrived and informed him smilingly, "I have a present for you."

The oranges, surely. Good old Victor!

Instead two other French officers came in, and with proper ceremony Thénault said, "In the name of the Republic I confer upon you le Médaille Militaire and la Croix de Guerre."

"For me?" Balsley asked, looking slightly frightened. "What for?" For the past couple of days he had watched several such ceremonies. The soldier was honored with medals and then he died. The preceding day he had seen two men get their medals. Each had died within the hour.

Thénault gently told Balsley he was given the two medals because he was suffering for France, the first seriously wounded American aviator.

"Merci," Balsley said in a frightened voice. "But I'm not going to die." When the officers left, he found he could only think of oranges.

Victor had not forgotten. Finding oranges was a little more difficult than finding a cow. He was ever available for his regular sorties as well as any other call to action. Although Victor had taken part in many combats, he had not yet "got his Boche." He was almost constantly in the air.

On the morning of June 23, 1916, the squadron had just returned from the nine-o'clock patrol without having encountered enemy planes. Victor was flying his new "bus," the Nieuport with the 110-horsepower engine. Coming in for a landing, he misjudged the height and bounced in so roughly that he snapped one of the thick rubber shock cords wrapped around the landing gear. His mechanic, Louis Bley, began working on the landing gear. He had barely started when they heard engines in the distance—and they were not those of French planes. Victor was all for taking off, despite the faulty landing gear.

Bley refused to help him start the plane, arguing that he might crash on the landing if he didn't while taking off.

Victor argued also, but Bley won. The German machines disappeared and Victor, laughing, went off to lunch while Bley finished repairing the plane.

There was another patrol scheduled for twelve-thirty. Thénault was to lead Norman Prince and the new man, Lufbery, on the sortie. Victor strode out of his quarters, which he shared with Kiffin, and proceeded to his gray Nieuport. Bley had fixed the landing gear and the ship was ready. In his big hands Victor carried a bundle of newspapers, some chocolate and a few oranges. How he got them no one ever knew.

Victor explained to Captain Thénault that he would tag along on the patrol and then drop off near Vadelaincourt to deliver the oranges and other things to Balsley. "I think there is little hope of saving him," he added.

He was trailing three Nieuports on the patrol when they reached the lines. From time to time the Captain glanced over his shoulder, where he could see Victor's plane. He was disturbed that he had not been able to get Victor into the hospital.

Thénault's thoughts were interrupted by bursts of antiaircraft shells near Verdun. There were two German observation planes below them, perhaps directing artillery fire upon the French. Signaling to Norman and Lufbery, the Captain pounced down on the German planes. As they were almost within firing range, three Fokkers jumped on them out of the sun. No point in committing suicide, Thénault reasoned. He waved to Norman and Lufbery and dived away from the slower Fokkers. They were too heavily outnumbered, three against five Germans. Their Nieuports carried a single gun and most of the German planes by then each carried two.

They were inside the German lines by about two miles. The Captain led the two Nieuports back toward Verdun. In the excitement he had forgotten about Victor. He twisted his neck, studying the sky, and saw nothing. By now Victor should have landed at the hospital. Completing their patrol, the three Nieuports returned to Behonne. Victor was not there.

Victor had been around 10,000 feet behind and above the planes of the Captain, Prince and Lufbery. He was pleased that he had been able to get the oranges for poor Balsley. Then he saw the Captain's plane leading Norman and Lufbery down upon two German observation planes. Next he saw the three Fokkers spring out of the sun upon his squadron mates. They had not seen Victor because he was behind and above the French formation.

Victor reacted as he always did: he pushed the stick forward and nosed down upon the attacking Fokkers. They scattered in surprise and the two-seaters dived away.

The Fokkers then reformed and concentrated upon Victor. He was caught in a shattering crossfire as the three planes came in from all sides. The Nieuport jerked into a nose-down attitude and then from 10,000 feet plunged straight down. About halfway the wings ripped from the fuselage, fluttering end over end in the brilliant blue sky. The rest of the plane, with its heavy motor in the nose, smashed into the ground behind the German lines not far from Beaumont.

Victor Chapman was the first of the American squadron to die. Though he had crashed inside the German positions a French observation plane had witnessed the fight. He phoned Thénault to inform him of Victor's death.

"Our grief was extreme," the Captain wrote to Victor's father, "for we loved him deeply. At the moments of greatest danger in the air we could always discover the silhouette of his machine, that machine which he managed with so much ease. One of my *pilotes* has just said to me, 'Would that I had fallen instead of him.' "

In France and America services were held for Victor, a great outpouring of genuine grief, patriotism and affection. Victor's own sentiments were best expressed by Kiffin Rockwell, who wrote to Mrs. John Jay Chapman. It was almost as if Victor had written himself.

He died the most glorious death and at the most glorious time of life to die, especially for him, with his ideals. I have never once regretted it for him, as I know he was willing and satisfied to give his life that way if it was necessary, and that he had no fear of death. It is for you, his father, relatives, myself, and for all who have known him, and the world as a whole, I regret the loss.

Yet he is not dead; he lives forever in every place he has been, and in every one who knew him, and in future generations little points of his character will be passed along. He is alive every day in this escadrille *and has tremendous influence on all our actions. even the* mécaniciens *do their work better and more conscientiously. And a number of times I have seen Victor's* mécanicien *standing and gazing off in the direction of where he saw Victor leaving for the lines.*

Louis Bley found it difficult to believe that Victor would never return. On the day Victor was killed, even after the news had come in by phone, Bley refused to leave the field. He waited, watching an empty sky which grew dark as the sun went down.

But Victor did not return. With tear-streaked face, his shoulders heaving with the sobs he could not conceal, Louis Bley walked away from the field.

7 ENTER LUF

Verdun brought home the meaning of war to the men in the *Escadrille Américaine.* Even the romantic skies had become deadly; the men were tired, some were even frightened and none could visualize an end to it. How far-sighted it had been of the French to send the new men! They were needed, for the two or three patrols a day took their toll. The freezing air at high altitudes, the need always to be on the alert, the battles, the further hazards of engines conking out or guns jamming—all combined to chip away at one's nerves.

Elliot Cowdin was the first to succumb to this wear and tear. As one of the original seven Americans, Cowdin had served more than a year. He had been in the Ambulance Service, then with a bomber squadron and with two fighter squadrons before he joined the *Escadrille Américaine.* Just two days after Victor "went west" (the term pilots used when one of their number was killed), Elliot had to be relieved of duties. Long hours in the air and tension-filled encounters with countless German planes had exhausted him emotionally. Late in June Elliot Cowdin left the squadron.

With Bill Thaw and Clyde Balsley in the hospital, with Victor dead and Elliot gone, Thénault had to depend upon the remaining "old-timers"—Kiffin, Mac, Bert Hall and Norman Prince—to initiate the new arrivals.

Of these, the most interesting were the two Frenchmen-turned-American who had just arrived. Didier Masson, who gave his home as Los Angeles, had been born in France. He was one of the first barnstormers, those pilots who in the early years of the century flew about the United States in rickety Curtiss or Wright planes giving exhibition flights. Masson was, in 1913, the Chief of the Mexican Air Service. He was also the entire Mexican Air Service, which consisted of one plane and one pilot. This was during the Mexican Revolution. With the outbreak of war in Europe, Masson resigned and left for France. He served first in the infantry, later transferring to the Air Service. An expert as well as an experienced pilot, Didier Masson also served as an instructor before he asked to be sent to the American Squadron at Verdun in mid-June 1916.

The other French-American, Gervaise Raoul Lufbery, was as stolid as he was silent. His father was an American who had lived in France and had married a French girl who died when Raoul was a year old. With two older brothers, he had been left in his grandmother's care while his father returned to Wallingford, Connecticut, hoping to fare better in his homeland.

Raoul Lufbery, Ace of the Lafaye
U. S. Air F

Edward Lufbery remarried in America; when his second wife died he was left with five children. To help his father, Raoul, by then in his teens, went to work in a chocolate factory and sent most of his earnings to his father in America.

Raoul was a sturdy, adventurous boy; he set out to see the world when he was nineteen. Taking any job that came along—from waiting on tables to working on a ship—he saw North Africa, the Balkans and Germany before, after three years of wandering, he decided to visit his father in America.

They were never to see each other. On the day Raoul arrived, his father, then a stamp dealer, went to Europe. He had not known of Raoul's intentions and had left on a buying trip. Raoul remained in Wallingford for almost two years before he was once again bitten by the travel bug. In New Orleans he worked as a baker, in San Francisco he was a waiter. Raoul then enlisted for a hitch in the United States Army—which automatically made him a United States citizen—and was stationed for almost two years in the Philippines.

When his enlistment expired Raoul decided to see the Orient and made his way to Japan and China. His travels and his various occupations made him self-reliant; he was able to speak several languages; he could tackle almost any job and do it. And he was tough.

It was while Raoul was working as a railroad ticket agent in Bombay, India, that he revealed one of his characteristics. When one of the city's most influential businessmen scolded Raoul for not having addressed him as *sir,* the businessman soon found himself flat on the floor of the station. His jaw ached and his dignity was impaired, to say the least.

Raoul next appeared in Calcutta. There, in 1912, he met Marc Pourpe, a famous exhibition flyer, then on tour through India. When it was obvious that Pourpe was in difficulty with the Indians hired to raise the canvas hangar, Lufbery took over and found himself a job.

As usual, he did a little of everything and quickly made himself indispensable. Pourpe was flying the tricky Bleriot, and when his regular mechanic became ill and returned to France, Raoul took over as Pourpe's *mécanicien*. The two young adventurers became devoted friends and traveled throughout the East demonstrating the mysteries of flight. Pourpe then made a historic flight, a round trip between Cairo and Khartoum. Lufbery contributed by traveling ahead to be certain the plane was properly serviced along the route.

Following this feat, in the summer of 1914 Pourpe and Lufbery returned to France to get a new plane. Their plan was to return to the Orient, but the coming of war canceled that.

As one of France's most celebrated airmen Pourpe was immediately accepted into the French Air Service. Raoul enlisted in the Foreign Legion and, thanks to Pourpe's influence, was transferred to Pourpe's squadron to serve as his personal mechanic. It was a perfect arrangement and both were happy with it. But Pourpe died in a crash in December 1914.

Despondent over the death of his friend, Raoul requested a transfer to aviator's school. He was sent to the school at Chartres, where he was taught to fly the Farman and Voisin bombers. He piloted Voisins at the Front in Escadrille V.B. 106 for about six months before he requested training as a *pilote de chasse*. Curiously—in the light of his future history—Lufbery was considered poor Nieuport pilot material and nearly failed. His instructors found him too rough on the *Bébé* and were considering sending him back to the "trucks."

But slowly, persistently, without any display of emotion, Lufbery made himself a skilled fighter pilot by sheer strength of will. He was cautious, he was methodical and he was in no hurry.

This was obvious when Luf, as he soon came to be called by the other pilots, came to join them at Verdun. He flew his regular patrols without the slightest trace of showmanship, little of the dash so typical of some of the other Americans. He was, at thirty-one, the oldest member of the squadron. "He kept his real self shut up like a clam in a shell," his squadron mate Edwin Parsons wrote. "He was a man seemingly devoid of fear or, in fact, emotion of any kind. But what a man he was in the air!"

An expert *mécanicien*, Luf was able to make certain that his engine was always in top form. He also understood his guns and checked each cartridge before it went into his machine-gun feed belt. In this manner he was able to eliminate gun-jamming. He also made himself an expert marksman. He was not an advocate of the headlong plunge, as Victor had been, as Kiffin was; Luf was very patient. Several weeks went by, and although he had told the men little about himself, they had come to like him as a dependable member of the unit. But there was nothing spectacular about Lufbery.

In striking contrast to Lufbery was Charles Nungesser, one of France's most colorful fighter pilots. Just why he reported in at N. 124 early in July 1916 is difficult to explain. After a series of spectacular air battles and crashes, Nungesser had been grounded and sent to a hospital. His handsome face was scarred, his ready smile was flashing—with a double row of gold teeth to replace his own, which had been knocked out in a crash. Both legs had been broken in a recent accident, so Nungesser had to use a cane to walk and was lifted into his Nieuport by his *mécaniciens*.

When he arrived at Behonne near Verdun to join the American squadron, Nungesser had nine enemy aircraft to his official credit— three times the number credited to the entire *Escadrille Américaine*. For several weeks after the death of Victor Chapman it seemed that the squadron could not snap out of its depression. Nungesser, supposedly on convalescent leave, dropped in out of the skies and attached himself to the squadron. Because he was a celebrity who was adored and mobbed everywhere he went, Nungesser was able to do pretty much as he pleased. He may have been sent to bolster the morale of the Americans, although this was not officially stated.

Whatever the reason for Nungesser's unexpected appearance, his presence made a difference. One day he set out in his Nieuport and with typical abandon jumped two German aircraft flying near Verdun. One, an Aviatik reconnaissance plane, was armed with two guns, as was its protective Fokker. Nungesser blazed in on the Aviatik and shot it down; the Fokker dived for the safety of the German lines. The pilot may well have recognized Nungesser's personal insignia painted on the sides of his plane: a black heart in which a death's head, coffin and candles were arranged in a weird design.

The Aviatik was Nungesser's tenth official victory and the American squadron's fourth—as well as the first since Bill Thaw's almost two months before.

Bert Hall, who was rapidly becoming the squadron's most unpopular member because of his loud-mouthed boastfulness, a tendency to cheat at cards and other dishonest acts, was the next to score. Two days after Nungesser's victory, Bert knocked down a Fokker, "one of the new type . . . fighters, all decorated up like a saloon," according to Bert's own description.

As the two planes fenced in the air, it became clear—even to Bert, who rarely missed the opportunity to enlarge upon an incident—that he had tangled with "a beginner, or a very nervous pilot." It was a matter of thrust and parry until Bert could get on the German's tail. Two short bursts and the plane flipped on its back, fell nose downward and spun 10,000 feet to the ground. Four days later De Laage, leading Prince and Rockwell, surprised a German two-seater just north of Fort Douaumont, one of the most famous of the Verdun forts, and shot the plane down. Rockwell probably scored, but there was no confirmation. Still, since Nungesser started the streak they had doubled the squadron score, which now stood at six official victories.

Then Raoul Lufbery was ready to show what he could do.

On July 31, 1916, Luf had taken off on a lone patrol around lunchtime. He was cruising over Etain, a few miles to the east of Verdun inside the German lines, when he spotted a German two-seater below. Luf climbed to get himself between the German plane and the sun. At the same time he carefully scanned the skies to be certain he wasn't being set up for a surprise attack by Fokkers. Fairly sure that just he and the unwary two-seater were alone in the sky, Luf dived.

The observer opened up with his machine guns as soon as Luf was within range. Luf held his fire, then spattered out a few rounds. The German pilot kicked the big two-seater out of the way, then tried to pull around to get his forward guns on Luf's Nieuport. Deftly Luf twisted the faster Nieuport out of the German's path and darted onto his tail again.

With speedy care Luf judged that the two-seater was in line with his Lewis gun on the upper wing. He released a steady stream of fire. The big plane seemed to stagger in the air; slowly it described a graceful turn onto its back and flame shot out of the fuselage. It fell to earth, sending up a great sheet of flame when it struck.

That was Lufbery's first official victory. Four days afterward Luf surprised a number of reconnaissance planes in practically the same spot and shot down two of them, one following almost directly after the other. Two planes in a single combat was remarkable enough, but that they were two-seaters was extraordinary. In a two-seater the pilot could attend to the flying and the observer could man the guns, while in a single-seater, the pilot did both. A further complication was the clumsy gun of the Nieuport at that time, with its capacity of only forty-seven rounds. But Luf was so skilled a pilot and hunter that even in a double-victory combat he didn't exhaust all his ammunition.

On August 8, four days after the double, Luf and McConnell had been sent out to protect French observation planes which were directing artillery fire from the air. They became separated when they flew through some clouds and Mac found himself alone over the French planes.

High above all of this Luf had spied an Aviatik heading for the French positions. It could have been on a photographing mission, or perhaps the aircraft was loaded with bombs. Determined to stop it, Luf climbed above the Aviatik. Neither the pilot nor the observer-gunner saw him as he stalked their plane. When he was dead sure he was in the proper spot for the attack, Luf dived.

Meanwhile Mac flew over the French planes, wondering what had become of Luf. As he turned to circle back toward Verdun, he was astonished to see an Aviatik coming toward him upside down. Mac saw that "it showed its white belly for an instant, then seemed to straighten out. Then it glided earthward in big zig-zags. . . . Just as I was going down to see where it landed, I saw it skimming across a field. It was outlined against the shell-wracked earth like a tiny insect until, just northwest of Fort Douaumont, it crashed upon the battlefield. A sheet of flame and smoke shot up from the tangled wreckage. I watched it burn, then I went back to my observation machines."

"Those poor fellows" was Luf's most revealing comment. Within a week he was to be awarded the *Médaille Militaire* and the *Croix de Guerre* with palm. By this time Nungesser had left the Escadrille to return to his own unit.

Another American, Paul Pavelka, joined the squadron at this time. A farmboy from Madison, Connecticut, Pavelka too had seen much of the world from an early age. He had been a cook in a sheep camp, a cowboy and a seaman. This last occupation gave him his nickname "Skipper" and his means of transportation to Europe when war broke out. Pavelka worked his way across the Atlantic with a boatload of horses. Upon arrival he enlisted in the French Foreign Legion. It was Pavelka who paused a second over the wounded form of Kiffin Rockwell on that day when Kiffin had been wounded in a bayonet charge. About a month later Pavelka was himself wounded in a frightful hand-to-hand fight in the trenches. On recovering from his wound, Pavelka elected to switch to aviation, as had so many other Americans.

Skipper Pavelka was a real adventurer in the best sense of the word. Like Lufbery, he had an affinity for action and the ability to take care of himself by quick thinking and cool performance. This was proved on one of his first patrols, when he had to face the most dreaded enemy of any airman: fire in the air.

He was flying at 9000 feet over Verdun when, as was their unfortunate wont, the engine suddenly burst into flame. This was a frequent hazard which the airmen dealt with in one of two ways, neither very pleasant. The pilot could simply step out of the cockpit and fall a mile or so through space to a fast merciful end, or he could stay with the plane, hoping he would not burn to death before he reached the ground. Because the planes were made primarily of wood and covered with painted fabric, they burned like tinder.

The rotary engines burned easily; all that was needed was a break in one of the pipes which carried the fuel into the cylinders and the interior of the cowling would be sprayed with gas. The instant it touched the hot, whirling cylinders it burst into flame.

Pavelka found himself confronted with this dread situation almost two miles above the ground. He watched with cold horror as flame and black smoke, fanned by the speed of the Nieuport, poured back at him. Skipper acted almost instinctively; he flipped off the ignition and closed the throttle. The problem was to keep the flames away from the cockpit and away from the fuel tank, located almost directly behind the engine. If that blew, he would descend in fiery fragments.

He tipped the Nieuport onto its side and dropped it down toward the earth with breathtaking speed. In this way the air pushed the flame to the side, keeping it from traveling too quickly back along the fuselage. This took only a matter of seconds, but even in this short time fire was devouring the plane. Charred fabric ripped off the wings as a sheet of flame licked at it. Blackened ribs began to show through and soon there would be no wing at all.

In a few seconds Skipper had side-slipped the Nieuport, trailing a boiling black curl of smoke and red-and-orange flame, from 9000 feet to just fifty feet above the ground. Not wishing to crash sideways into the ground, he had to right the plane and find a place to land. The heat roared back toward him, curling the fuselage fabric and scorching Pavelka's face and hands. Now at least all of the front half of the plane was blazing.

Seeing he was over a swamp, which would be both damp and soft, Skipper pulled back on the stick and threw the plane into a stall. This dropped the flying inferno right into the swamp. As soon as he felt the jar of the impact, Skipper yanked away his seat belt and leaped from the flames into the ooze of the swamp.

He rose, blissfully covered with mud, and ran from the blazing wreckage. He had covered barely 150 feet when the flames reached the fuel tank. The plane disappeared in a burst of orange, red and black. Thrown into the mud by the concussion of the explosion, Skipper was unhurt except for some facial burns and blistered hands.

But not quite safe. German artillery opened up on the column of smoke rising from the swamp, and heavy shells began cracking around the harassed Pavelka. But, old infantryman that he was and having survived by some miracle so fiery a fall from the sky, he was hardly ruffled. Ignoring the barrage, Skipper calmly walked out of the swamp toward the French lines. After all he had experienced, he was certain the German guns couldn't touch him. He made the French lines without further injury.

Meanwhile Norman Prince was brooding. Everyone seemed to have had adventures or accounted for "his Hun" except Norman. As the originator of the squadron, Norman somehow felt that he deserved to win some sort of glory. He flew on all the patrols, came home with bulletholes in his plane, but he seemed immune to German bullets. The Germans were also immune to his. Or else he had bad luck—engine trouble or jammed guns. Something always went wrong.

Here it was August 1916; they had been at Verdun for almost four months. The squadron score stood at ten confirmed victories. Only a plane actually seen to fall and burn or crash was credited to the man who brought it down. In addition, witnesses on the ground had to back up the claim—the man's own squadron mates would not do. Not one of the ten planes to the squadron's credit had been knocked down by Norman, and he was not happy about it. It was as if fate had turned against him.

One day he was flying alone several miles inside the German lines when he sighted a single two-seater Aviatik a couple of thousand feet below him regulating artillery fire upon the French positions. It looked like a trap, for the Germans generally liked to put a lone plane out hoping to attract a lone pilot or a small patrol and then swoop down out of the sun with a number of

The wreckage of a German observation plane shot down over Verdun, 1916.

U. S. Air Force Pho

Fokkers. Quickly scanning the sky around him, Norman was almost certain there were no enemy planes around except the Aviatik. Besides, he wanted to get that plane.

Down he went in a screaming dive, past the Aviatik, then he gently pulled back on the stick and was almost directly behind and just under the tail. He pulled the trigger release and poured a stream of fire into the German plane. Norman pulled the Nieuport around and saw that his first attack had killed the observer in the rear cockpit. When the German pilot attempted to dive away, Norman, in the faster Nieuport, stuck to his tail, blasting away at the virtually helpless plane. The pilot could fight back only if Norman permitted himself to get in front of the Aviatik's forward-firing gun.

Finally, his plane full of holes and Norman flitting around like a hornet, the German pilot raised his hands above his head. Here was a strange situation. Norman was more than six miles inside the German lines and he had a prize in his hand. He could have shot the plane down, but who would have seen it fall? He would never get that victory confirmed.

Norman pulled alongside the Aviatik and pointed west, toward the French positions. The German pilot nodded and turned the plane for Verdun. Any time he seemed to get off course, Norman reminded him a little by firing a burst from his Lewis gun. When they were near Verdun, Norman pointed down and the German set the Aviatik in a meadow and the plane was soon swarming with French soldiers. It was the first intact German plane brought down by an American inside the French lines. For this exploit Norman was awarded the *Médaille Militaire*. Even more important, it ended his streak of bad luck.

In September the squadron had received its orders to leave Verdun—the battle there having died out from sheer waste of human life—and were ready to leave by the ninth. The weather had held them down a great deal since Norman's exploit, but on the morning of September 9, Kiffin had attacked a two-seater. He had killed the observer and followed the plane down until attacked by two Fokkers. Wisely he broke away without being certain that his battle had accomplished anything. When he arrived back at the field he was greeted with the news that French ground observers had seen the two-seater crash—Kiffin's second "official."

Not to be outdone, Norman went out that afternoon and came upon a flight of three Fokkers. Having the advantage of height and the sun, Norman pounced.

His silver Nieuport almost touched the last plane in the formation before Norman's Lewis gun chattered. Norman knew it was suicide to mix with the numbers against him and continued his dive for the French lines. He looked over his shoulder as he went and saw the Fokker he had attacked in a death dive. When he landed at Behonne, he learned that he had won his second official. The squadron score now stood at thirteen.

The squadron was closing its chapter at Verdun with some proud pages. Bill Thaw had been able to rejoin them, though his arm was still in a cast.

Unfortunately, Mac McConnell, the other promising eagle, "a pilot as modest as he was brave," in the words of one of his citations, had his own run of ill fortune. On one of the patrols he flew with Kiffin and Norman, Mac remained over the battlefield until after nightfall. When the three planes turned toward home the stars were beginning to twinkle.

Norman and Kiffin had managed to set down safely on the darkened field but when Mac came in he was too late. He lost sight of Behonne and began anxiously seeking some other field in which to land.

"I made for a field," he wrote, "but in the darkness I couldn't judge my distance well and went too far. At the edge of the field there were trees, and beyond, a deep cut where a road ran." Coming in at high speed, Mac used up most of the landing space even before the Nieuport hit the ground. The plane continued racing for the trees.

Mac threw his arms over his face as he saw two large trees loom

A Nieuport after a bad landing.

up in the dark. The Nieuport plowed through them, leaving its wings wrapped around the tree trunks. The rest of the plane shot ahead and didn't stop until it struck the side of the road bank. The tail whipped up and was severed by telephone wires that ran along the road. Mac was still inside the cockpit, hanging head down, when the *poilus* ran up to pull him out. Although when he wrote home Mac had said "I wasn't even bruised," the crash had wrenched his back seriously.

Not admitting that he was in great pain, Mac continued flying in planes he borrowed from the other pilots. Even so, he could only get into the cockpit with help from two men. Noting this, Captain Thénault sent Mac with Kiffin to Paris on leave. There the pain in his back was so intense that Mac couldn't sleep and had to rest sitting up. Kiffin even had to help him dress. What Mac did not know was that rheumatism had settled in his back. When he returned to the squadron, despite his arguments the Captain had him committed to a hospital.

Mac was therefore not with the squadron when it finally was ordered to leave the Verdun sector. There was great excitement as the men prepared to move again. They would leave their *Bébé* Nieuports behind, for they were to be issued the new Model 17, which was slightly larger and came armed with a fuselage-mounted Vickers gun which fired directly through the propeller arc. This was exciting news in itself.

Even more exciting was the fact that they were to be granted leave in Paris. All except Luf, who had talked the Captain into letting him go to Chartres, where he knew a girl.

The rest of the squadron descended upon Paris for what the English call "fun and games." They had free access to the home of Dr. Gros as well as that of the Bostonian Alice Weeks, whose son had been killed serving in the Foreign Legion. Mrs. Weeks found consolation in the high spirits and eager laughter of the young Americans who luxuriated in the warm atmosphere of her home.

But she had not counted upon Whiskey.

The boys had run across a newspaper advertisement in the pet section which struck their collective eye. The Captain had his German Shepherd Fram, so why not a companion for Fram?

Several of the pilots pooled their money and answered the ad. Whiskey, for that was the name bestowed upon their mascot, cost no less than 500 francs. He caused immediate trouble in Mrs. Weeks' house when he surprised one of the maids, who ran shrieking.

Whiskey was a lion cub. Though about the size of a small dog and not very good at roaring like the proper King of Beasts, Whiskey caused excitement, even consternation, everywhere he went. And he went everywhere.

Consequently, depending upon the local attitude toward lions, the men of the squadron were either the center of attention or else were thrown out of restaurants or off trains. Whiskey was a most affectionate pet, and though he was especially fond of Bill Thaw, his nursemaid during most of the Paris stay, Whiskey

loved Raoul Lufbery. In time another cub joined the household
(or rather the squadron roster, for the presence of Whiskey made
the *Escadrille Américaine* one of the most talked-about on the
Front), a lady lion cub.

Needless to say, she was promptly named Soda. Female lions
tend to take their occupation more seriously than the generally
lazy males. Soda was therefore not quite so friendly as Whiskey,
who "didn't know he was a lion and thought he was just another
dog," in Lufbery's description. Soda would spit and claw; Whiskey loved to be petted. Only Luf, in time, was permitted to approach her.

Soda and Whiskey, the official mascots of the Lafayette Escadrille.

8 "...FOR LAFAYETTE..."

Luf always could get along better with lions than with railroad employees. Captain Thénault learned that quickly enough. While the others were going about their merry way in Paris Luf had an "incident."

Because he had taken an unofficial leave (the Captain was always willing to blink a bit when his men bent a regulation or two), Lufbery had no leave papers when he went off to Chartres.

On the train he encountered a quite stuffy conductor who insisted upon seeing not only Luf's ticket, but also his papers. Not wanting to get either himself or the Captain in trouble, Luf refused to comply. The conductor laid a hand on Luf, which was a mistake. Luf did not like to be touched. He laid a hand on the conductor—right in the mouth, and six teeth came out.

Now he was in the soup. As Luf languished in jail, Thénault was ordered to get in touch with the military officials in Chartres.

"I found at the other end of the wire," Thénault reported after he phoned, "an old general—very irritated." Thénault was able to smooth the old man's ruffled military feathers. Since, technically, Luf was an American volunteer fighting for France, that made an impression; also Luf had four German planes to his credit—one more and he would be an Ace. Certainly the general would not wish to jail so aggressive a fighter. France would certainly be the loser. The general sighed but agreed. Luf hurried to Paris to join the rest of the squadron and Whiskey.

There had been much discussion as to their next station. Since the hard fighting had switched from Verdun to the Somme, where the British were on the offensive, they were certain they would go there.

There was some disappointment when Captain Thénault informed them that on September 17 they would return to Luxeuil, the peaceful sector in which they had begun operations six months before. The trip from Paris to Luxeuil by train was uneventful, except that Bill Thaw was thrown off the train because of his "African dog." He arrived at the field a day late, having arranged for Whiskey to travel in a crate.

The once almost-lazy field at Luxeuil had changed since they left. New hangars had been put up and the field buzzed with strange new aircraft, British to judge from the insignia. They were Sopwith One-and-a-Half Strutters—large two-seater biplanes which served as fighter-reconnaissance aircraft. These graceful planes were also used as day bombers by the Royal Naval

Air Service, whose Number Three Wing was now stationed at. Luxeuil. Most of the pilots were Canadians.

Luxeuil was also the home base of the French Groupe de Bombardment No. 4 under the tough Captain Félix Happe. His men piloted the already-obsolescent Farmans and Bréguet-Michelins. The energetic, fiery Happe hinted at great plans in the wind but told Thénault nothing definite. It was a letdown. Worse, their new planes had not arrived and the entire squadron was grounded. In the hospital Mac was quite surprised to get letters, not about air combat but about Bill Thaw's prowess as a trout fisherman and Lufbery's love for gathering mushrooms. There were stories about how the Americans and Canadians hit it off well and took turns throwing parties for each other. As often as not the parties reached a climax of good-natured high jinks in which the host's dining room, and all his crockery, were left a shambles. Like big bear cubs, the young aviators wrestled, threw things, laughed and generally blew off steam to soothe their strained nerves.

Although they were young, eager, vigorous, they were not supermen. Their kind of "work" took its toll, even if they were never completely aware of the fact. Kiffin Rockwell, who seemed always to be in the air seeking combat, even admitted this. "Am tired out now"; he wrote to his brother Paul, "have been out four different times today, all the time going up and down. Once I dropped straight down from 4000 meters to 1800 on a Boche, but he got away. It tires one a lot—the changes in heights and the maneuvering."

At Verdun, Kiffin had appeared to be tireless. He was constantly on patrol, either with other squadron members or alone. When his friends tried to caution him against the continual grind or his headlong courage, Kiffin, eyes flashing, replied, "I pay my part for Lafayette and Rochambeau!" These two Frenchmen had fought on the American side during the Revolution; so had one of Kiffin's ancestors.

During July Kiffin had taken part in no fewer than forty aerial combats; in August he fought thirty-four battles. The strain took its toll and his youthful face was seamed; though not quite twenty-four he appeared older. His tall, slender frame was even thinner.

The enforced rest at Luxeuil helped. Kiffin hiked through the lovely French countryside; he read or wrote letters to his brother Paul. He enjoyed talking with the British pilots stationed at the field and studying their Sopwith Strutter, so named because of the unusual arrangement of struts which fastened to the center section of the wing just over the fuselage. (Two very long ones on each side, with two short struts that joined in the middle of the wing, accounted for the name the pilots had given to the bomber. Though called The One-and-a-Half-Strutter, they quickly shortened it simply to "Strutter.")

Kiffin Rockwell in his Bébé Nieuport *checking his machine gun, which is mounted on t of the upper wing. At far left a mechanic prepares a drum of ammunition.*

Courtesy Paul Rockw

All the activity on the field stirred Kiffin. He became impatient
and restless, hoping that the Nieuports would arrive soon. He
heard, too, from pilots of the other fighter squadrons based in the
vicinity that the Germans were sending up plenty of Fokkers,
both the old monoplanes and some new biplanes. The enemy
was also expecting something to come out of all the hustle and
bustle at Luxeuil.

The German reconnaissance planes which passed over the field
could spot the activity, see the new hangars and the dug-in gun
positions. From time to time they would send over some bombers
to discourage the builders. Not all the German planes had been
sent up to the Battle of the Somme, obviously.

Finally after a few days five new Nieuports arrived. They were
the model 17C–1 (the *C* designating "Chaser" or pursuit plane,
and the *1* that it was a single-seater), somewhat larger than the
model 11s the squadron had been flying. The new plane was,
however, a great deal more powerful—it could climb to 7000 feet
in six minutes. And instead of the awkward forty-seven-shot
Lewis gun mounted on the top of the wing, it was armed with a
Vickers placed directly in front of the pilot, slightly to the left,

on the fuselage, geared to fire directly through the revolving propeller. It was belt-fed, which meant that instead of using a round
canlike container of bullets, the bullets were on a belt which
passed through the gun breech. It carried 500 rounds of ammunition, a marked advantage over the canister. The new model was
also about ten miles an hour faster than the old *Bébé*.

As soon as the planes arrived the mechanics began to assemble
them and to mount the gun. Some pilots, not trusting the single
Vickers, continued to have the additional Lewis weapon on the
upper wing.

There were eleven pilots on the ready roster, not counting
the Captain and De Laage. While they were in Paris, another
Rockwell—Robert Lockerbie Rockwell—from Cincinnati,
Ohio, joined them. A prewar medical student, he had served
earlier in the war as an interne at the Anglo-American Hospital
in Paris and at a French Hospital in Saint-Valery-on-Caux.
"Doc," as he was inevitably called by his squadron mates, had
been a pilot before the war and had no trouble proving himself
a proficient pilot before being sent to join N. 124.

Still there were eleven pilots and five planes. And preparing
the craft for combat took time. Within three days of the delivery
only two planes were assembled and gunned; these were assigned to Kiffin and Luf. There was one additional problem—
because of the fighting on the Somme, there was an ammunition
shortage. Only enough rounds were on hand to fill two ammunition belts. These were installed in the two ready planes. The next
day, Thénault promised—if the weather was good—the impatient Luf and Kiffin could take a morning patrol.

That evening, as he sat with Paul Pavelka, Kiffin was unusually
thoughtful. "Paul," he said, "if I'm shot down, I want to be
buried where I fall."

This shocked Pavelka, for he had always found Kiffin hopeful
and not given over to morbidity. There was always the possibility
of being shot down, of course, but few talked about it. They discussed ways of not being shot down. Maybe Kiffin was still over-
tired after Verdun.

The next morning, September 23, 1916, was crisp and sunny. Kiffin and Luf were eager to test their new Nieuports. They were driven over to the field from their quarters and ready to go before the sun tipped the edges of the Vosges Mountains.

Kiffin's plane left the ground first, followed by Luf's. They climbed and flew west toward the mountains. Soon they were over the peak called the Hartsmanwillerkopf, flying in the high cold air. Just below them they saw some Fokkers, inside the French lines and heading for home—either to Colmar or Habsheim, which were thick with Fokkers.

The two Nieuports dived down upon the German planes and prepared to fire. Luf arrived first, only to suffer a characteristic misfortune with the gun. His nice new Vickers jammed on the first burst. Kicking the rudder and jamming the stick to the side, Luf pulled away from the battle. He began hammering away at the Vickers but could not clear the jam.

Luckily, Kiffin had realized Luf was in trouble and had not mixed with the Fokkers, which were now well inside the German lines. He guided his Nieuport up close to Luf's and exchanged hand signals. Luf pointed down in the direction of Fontain, where there was a French airfield. Rather than fly all the way back to Luxeuil, he would drop in on the Frenchmen and have the jammed gun cleared, take on some more fuel and continue the patrol.

Kiffin escorted Luf, who would have been helpless if attacked, to the field. Then, as Luf spiraled down for a landing, Kiffin waved goodbye and turned back for the lines. Evidently he hoped a stray Fokker might still be there.

Kiffin pulled the stick back and gained some altitude until he was in the cold clear air again. His eyes squinted through the goggles as he studied the sky. The engine roared steadily, with a fine powerful sound. Alone, Kiffin was in his element, happy in the brilliant blue of the hazardous sky. As with all experienced pilots, he kept his head in continual motion, sweeping the sky around, behind and above him.

Before he reached the lines he saw a German plane—a two-seater Aviatik similar to the one he had shot down in his first aerial combat four months before.

Kiffin reacted as he always did. He leaned forward, eye on the sight, and pushed the stick forward. The Nieuport plummeted down upon the Aviatik. Coolly, as was his practice, Kiffin held his fire even as he raced through the stream of lead pouring out of the rear gun of the German plane.

Down, down, down he went as the enemy gun stuttered and the tracers skittered around the diving Nieuport. The gap closed rapidly until it appeared to an observer on the ground that the two planes would have to smash in midair.

Frantically the German pilot kicked and joggled the Aviatik out of the path of Kiffin's Nieuport. There was a brief sputter from Kiffin's gun just before his plane raced past the Aviatik.

But to the watcher on the ground below, a French artillery captain with field glasses, something was wrong. The Nieuport continued in its dive until its speed increased beyond the danger point. With horror the French officer watched as a wing ripped away, which threw the Nieuport into a spin. Gyrating and disintegrating in the air, Kiffin's Nieuport shattered against the ground. He had fallen just inside the French lines, near the ruined village of Rodern, in a tiny field of flowers.

Immediately the German artillery guns opened up on the downed plane, but *poilus* from a friendly artillery battery rushed out to get the pilot. When Kiffin's body was brought into the comparative safety of a trench, it was found that he had been struck in the chest by an explosive bullet. Death must have occurred instantaneously two miles in the air just after he had fired a few rounds at the Aviatik. The examining surgeon said that had the bullet been the ordinary one, instead of the "unlawful" explosive bullet (which could only "legally" be used on balloons), Kiffin might have survived the wound.

But he had not. Kiffin Rockwell, the man who had been described as "the soul of the *Escadrille Américaine*," had given his life for France. He had paid his debt for Lafayette and Rochambeau.

*batros two-seater reconnaissance plane. A tough adversary because of the two-man team
pilot and gunner, it was this type of plane that Kiffin Rockwell attacked when he was
led.*

Meanwhile at the field of Escadrille N. 49, Luf waited while the mechanics cleared his gun and refueled the plane. From time to time, as he impatiently waited for the men to finish working on the Nieuport, he anxiously scanned the skies for a sign of Kiffin.

The phone rang in the squadron headquarters and he was told that his friend had just crashed to his death. Eyes blazing, his swarthy face gone suddenly pale, Luf ran from the building to his waiting plane. The engine had been started and he leaped into the cockpit. His eyes were glistening with tears as he gunned the engine; without waiting to reach a safe takeoff speed, Luf yanked back on the stick and took off as nearly vertically as was possible in a Nieuport.

Luf raced to the scene of the fight and began ranging across the sky looking for a German plane upon which he could avenge the death of Kiffin. He shouted in anger to find the sky empty. In his grief he became dangerously reckless, so unusual for Luf. He banked the Nieuport and kicked the rudder and headed into Germany. He found the field at Colmar, dived down upon it and swooped over the hangars—but no Fokkers came to challenge him. With a curse, Luf raced to Habsheim, where he again dared the Fokkers to come up, but with the same result.

When his fuel supply became dangerously low, Luf could do nothing but return to Luxeuil. There he joined the stricken pilots—De Laage, who had often flown with Kiffin in battle, was unashamedly sobbing. That Kiffin, who had been with them for so long and who better than anyone else represented that spirit which had gone into the squadron, was no more was simply un-believable. Victor's death had been hard to take, but he had seemed to seek out danger and death. Kiffin was courageous, but he had been more mature and it seemed he would never fall.

"When Rockwell was in the air," Captain Thénault said, "no Germans passed . . . and he was in the air most of the time.

"The best and bravest of us all is no more."

9 THE OBERNDORF MISSION

With Kiffin's death only three of the original seven members of the *Escadrille Américaine* were left in active service: Bill Thaw, Norman Prince and Bert Hall. James McConnell was still in the hospital with a bad back and Elliot Cowdin had been sent home. Only Bert seemed worried by the dwindling numbers, wondering who would be next.

Because of the slowness in delivery of their new planes and because of the shortage of ammunition, there was little for them to do. And though Captain Happe continued to promise a great bombing raid, which was why they had been brought back to Luxeuil, there seemed no definite date set for it.

September faded into October; boredom became their chief concern. A week went by and the men had become more resigned to Kiffin's absence. Then, suddenly, plenty of ammunition arrived at the field. Within hours, just the length of time it took to unload the crates and fill the machine-gun belts, Luf and Norman were ready to take off.

"To get some Germans for Kiffin," they said almost in unison.

Together they streaked for the Fokker nest at Mulhouse. In the clouds they became separated. Luf arrived over the German airfield first and, just as he had on the day Kiffin died, circled over the field daring the Germans to come up and fight. But nothing happened and he was forced to return to Luxeuil for fuel.

Once again, in the clouds, he and Norman missed each other. For just as he passed over Mulhouse, Norman ran into an angry bunch of Fokkers which had been stirred up by Luf. Norman was badly outnumbered and soon found himself little more than a flying target. The wisest course for him was to run, but even that was difficult, for there seemed to be a Fokker sputtering fire at him everywhere he turned. All around him swatches of fabric were torn away, then one of the center struts holding the wing to his plane's fuselage. An explosive bullet struck the leading edge of the lower right wing and split it.

If the Nieuport could hold together after all that, Norman knew he could outrun the Fokkers. There were no *ifs;* he had to run. Putting the plane in a shallow dive, he made for home.

Meanwhile, Luf had returned to Luxeuil and had his Nieuport refueled. When he learned that Norman had not yet come back, he sprinted for the plane. Would Norman suffer the same fate as Kiffin? And would it be because Luf had had to leave him alone? With these thoughts in his mind Lufbery sped toward Mulhouse.

He did not know that, shortly after he had taken off, a very shaken Norman Prince fluttered to earth in a battle-scarred Nieu-port. It would require a good deal of repair work, but it had held together long enough for the white-faced, stuttering Norman to get home safely.

Luf searched in vain for Norman, suspecting the worst. Instead he encountered a lone Fokker whose markings he recognized. They had dueled before. Luf worked around behind the German aircraft and then

I dive upon him, but with remarkable skill he gets out of range of my machine gun. He has anticipated my maneuver and parried the blow before it was struck. I am now aware that I have to do with a master of the art.

Making my machine tango from right to left, I saw him below me but much nearer than before by at least forty yards. Suddenly he noses up as if to begin a looping, and in this awkward position fires a volley at me which I dodge by a half turn to the right. A second time I attack but with no more success.

The wind carries us to the north of Mulhouse [deeper inside the German lines], *and I begin to ask myself if I am not playing my adversary's game for him in delaying longer.*

At this moment I chanced to glance in the direction of Belfort which was about twelve miles within our lines. I perceived in the air little white flakes [French antiaircraft bursts]. *Evidence of the presence of a Boche. A lucky chance! I had now an excuse for abandoning without loss of honor the match, which I am not at all sorry to leave. Only before leaving my adversary I feel I must show him that I appreciate that he is a valiant foe and respect him as such.*

Drawing my left arm out of the fuselage I waved him a sign of adieu. He understands and desires to show courtesy on his part, for he returns my farewell.

It was this kind of gentlemanly encounter, hungrily reported in newspapers or, as in this case the periodical *La Guerre Aerienne,* which made the war in the air so romantic to those who did not suffer its discomforts, cold, the effects of swift altitude changes, oxygen deficiency, fear and death. This knightly jousting high above the earth was, of course, much cleaner and less wholesale than the ugly war on the ground.

The next stage in Lufbery's adventures was more typical. He raced for Belfort and came upon a German two-seater obviously on a reconnaissance mission. Without taking his usual precautions, mainly because he hoped to bring down an enemy plane inside his own lines, Luf swooped down for the kill. At about fifty yards he opened up on the German. But then from behind and above him, someone had opened up on Luf. He had fallen for the oldest trap on the Front: a slow two-seater covered by a Fokker hiding in the sun.

The hunter had become the hunted. Luf ducked into his cockpit as scorching lead slugs spattered all around him. The Fokker was dancing its own tango as its twin Maxim machine guns sprayed the little Nieuport. Luf felt bullets striking his heavy flying suit; one went through his boot. Though his clothing was punctured Luf was himself miraculously untouched.

But his plane was in near-tatters: the fabric of the wing was torn, the left aileron was completely out of commission, the elevator was just barely staying in place. Worse: three slugs had smashed into the engine and another punctured the fuel tank. Lufbery's luck held, however, for the Fokker did not continue the fight, but hit and ran. They were too deep inside the French lines for a dogfight.

Luf, like Norman a half-hour earlier, had plenty of problems. His fuel gone, his engine out and his controls half shot away, he had to settle down to earth fast.

Sighting the nearest airdrome, Luf nursed the staggering Nieuport to the ground—an amazing demonstration of airmanship by a man who had almost been washed out as a student fighter pilot. When the Nieuport was examined it was found so badly damaged that it had to be junked.

"It had made its last flight!" Luf commented. "Poor *Coucou* [Baby]."

When he and Norman got together in the evening they admitted that instead of avenging Kiffin, they had almost joined him. But a couple of days later Norman surprised a Fokker in almost the same aerial battleground and succeeded in shooting it down. It was Norman's second official victory (the squadron's fourteenth); he was trailing Luf by two. Three more victories and Norman would become an Ace.

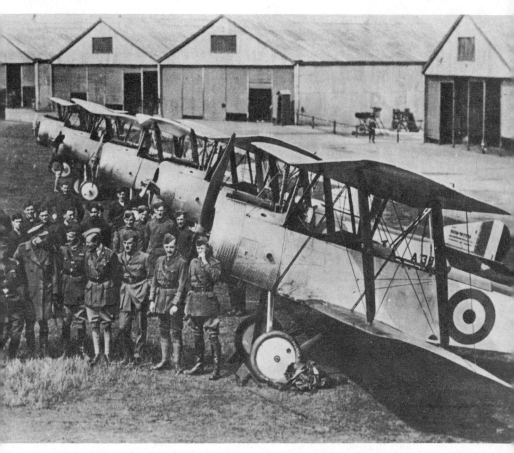

tish pilots and their Sopwith Strutters. Planes such as these were employed on the erndorf raid, October 1916.

U. S. Air Force Photo

On the night of October 11, 1916, the pilots were informed that the big bombing mission was to take place on the next day. At last some real action, this time deep inside Germany, for the British and French bombers had been ordered to bomb Oberndorf. Target: the Mauser factory in which rifles for the German Army were turned out.

Oberndorf lay almost directly east and slightly to the north of Luxeuil—a distance of 175 kilometers, which meant a round trip of more than 220 miles. This was a long flight for the bombers and would be one of the deepest penetrations of the war into Germany. However, the fighters with their smaller fuel capacity could escort the bombers only part of the way. They would have to turn back at some point, land, refuel and then be ready to join the returning bombers.

It was a complicated plan and one of history's first truly "strategic" bombing missions. That is, the mission was planned to have a long-range effect upon the war rather than an immediate one ("tactical" missions). The plan was not to knock a hole through some trenches but to destroy the enemy's ability to make war by wrecking his ability to make rifles. A successful mission could have a great impact upon the outcome of the war; it could even shorten it.

As with most such ambitious plans, much would go wrong.

Captain Happe found himself with an air armada of about forty planes, his own Farmans, Bréguet-Michelins, some borrowed Sopwith Strutters to serve as escort fighters, and the British Strutters of the Royal Navy Air Service, Number Three Wing. The excitable Happe had never commanded so imposing a force.

Not all of the Strutters carried bombs; some were to act as escorts for the bombers and would carry machine guns and serve as fighters instead. Happe was not especially pleased to learn that the American squadron would be able to contribute only five Nieuports to the big mission.

Captain Thénault had gone on leave a day or two before, leaving Alfred de Laage de Meux in command. Not a man to miss a good show, De Laage named himself as one of the escort pilots and selected to go with him Lufbery, Norman Prince and Didier Masson, one of the newer, though experienced, men.

Bert Hall was assigned the fifth plane to fly with another force of about eighteen on a diversionary mission to Lorrach, a German town just on the other side of the Rhine River, not far from the Swiss border and miles south of Oberndorf. It was hoped that this raid would draw the German fighters away from the day's real target.

The remaining Americans could only stand around and watch the great activity on the field at Luxeuil and then wait until late in the afternoon to learn what the results had been.

The air reverberated with the sound of engines; there was great shouting, the smell of fuel and much confusion. It was a typical October day, cold, with some clouds over the field. A reconnaissance plane had gone over into Germany, however, and reported visibility good. It would be a history-making mission.

The flight path would take the forty planes over the Front Lines, above the Vosges Mountains. They would cross the Rhine and continue more than fifty miles into Germany. Just beyond the Black Forest, on the Neckar River, lay Oberndorf. The path also crossed over the Fokker nest at Colmar; some fifty miles to the south was Habsheim.

Just short of the Black Forest the escorting Nieuports of N. 124 would have to leave their charges, the eight Bréguet-Michelins of B.M. 120.

The mission began around 1:15 P.M. when the first Farmans began struggling down the field on their takeoff run; the Strutters followed; and finally, the most lumbering of all, the Bréguet-Michelins managed to get into the air. By this time it was approaching two o'clock, clouds were forming and not many hours of daylight were left for the long flight ahead.

Trouble plagued the mission almost from the start. Of the first six Farmans to take off, two had to land almost immediately because of engine trouble; the remaining four continued on the mission. Of the second group of six Farmans, three dropped out before reaching the lines, two were shot down near the Rhine and the remaining plane dropped its bomb load upon Oberndorf, struggled back to France and crash-landed. Of the British units, one section of nine planes made it to Oberndorf, losing one Sopwith inside Germany. Another section of ten planes took off, but four turned back because of mechanical troubles before the lines were crossed. The remaining six planes continued into Germany, where they proceeded to bomb the wrong target, the city of Donaueschingen. On the return flight, two of these Bréguets were shot down and all four of the crew members taken prisoner.

Of the forty planes sent out, twenty-four actually bombed a target (even if six did bomb the wrong one); nine planes did not make it across the lines and ten planes never returned. The mission to Oberndorf was not a great success.

As for squadron B.M. 120, which the four Nieuports of the *Escadrille Américaine* escorted, it suffered the same fate as the others. Eight bombers took off, four reached Oberndorf and only three succeeded in making the round trip.

It was about 1:45 P.M. before the ungainly Bréguets got off the ground. The little Nieuports were forced to circle around them because the big bombers could barely reach a speed of sixty-five miles an hour. Just over the Vosges some of the first Fokkers appeared, one of them piloted by Ernst Udet, who had a single victory to his credit at the time. By the end of the war, Udet would be Germany's number-two Ace, with sixty-two "kills."

Udet was flying in a new Fokker biplane. He eluded the Nieuports, got behind one of the Bréguets, fired 350 rounds and put the engine out of commission. The plane came to earth at Rustenhart, between the Front Line and the Rhine.

"It landed intact," Udet reported, "and in order to prevent the occupants from destroying it, I landed beside it. Because my tires were punctured by shots, I turned over, but without serious consequences. It was a comical picture; the vanquished landed upright and the victor landed upside-down. Both Frenchmen clambered down and we shook hands all around."

Shortly after this fight, which none of the men in the Nieuports had apparently seen, the four planes had to turn back for fuel. The remaining seven bombers continued on. Three fell to German guns within the next few miles, so that only four continued on to the target to bomb the already-smoking Mauser factory. When they reached Oberndorf it was already three-thirty in the afternoon, and they had a long flight back. The autumn evening was beginning to fall when the Bréguets headed back for Luxeuil.

By then the Oberndorf mission had become a great air battle stretching across most of the flight path. German fighters darted in and out of the formations while machine-gun tracers crisscrossed the darkening sky. In the confusion of battle one witness saw a Strutter, in a fight with a Fokker, shoot down a Farman that had somehow flown into its sights. The hapless French plane blew up in the air and showered down in pieces.

The battle had grown furious just as the four Nieuports burst into the smoking aerial battlefield. Leading his little formation, De Laage spotted a Fokker on the tail of one of the bombers, struggling to weave out of the way. De Laage's bullets found their mark and the German plane dropped out of the battle. Masson threw his plane into a battle with an Aviatik. He got off fifty rounds and watched the Aviatik dropping through the clouds in a death spin.

There were enough targets to go around. Lufbery too attacked a German plane and brought it down. He became the first official Ace of the *Escadrille Américaine*. Nor was Norman Prince denied a victory. The battle had strayed out of the German sky and into France. The German planes, low on fuel and ammunition, began leaving the battle. Norman caught one of the last Fokkers before it turned away and raised his total to three planes; two more and he would be an Ace. Jubilant, he was ready to return home. Of the four planes from N. 124, he could find only Luf's still in the air.

De Laage had returned to Luxeuil; Masson with a nicked fuel tank had just managed to squeeze himself into the French lines, where he dropped his plane. He managed to get to the safety of the French trenches before German artillery destroyed the Nieuport.

Together Luf and Norman proceeded toward home. It had grown too dark to return to Luxeuil; by the time they arrived there it would have become too dark to land. Instead they selected a little forward field at Corcieux on which they could land. They could spend the night, no doubt celebrating their victories, and return to Luxeuil in the morning.

Luf led the way into the field. As they approached the earth the full darkness became more apparent. Luf carefully nursed his Nieuport to the ground and was swallowed up in the purple of nightfall. He quickly gunned the plane out of the way for Norman.

Gingerly Norman eased his Nieuport into the little landing field. He did not possess the vision of Luf (in fact, he had quite poor eyesight). He brought the plane in over the trees that edged the field and all seemed well. But in the darkness he failed to see some high-tension cables near treetop level.

The landing gear of the Nieuport struck the cable; the plane flipped into the ground on its nose with a grinding crash. The speed at which Norman had been coming in was great enough to propel the Nieuport end over end down the field.

With dread in his eyes Luf watched his friend's plane destroy itself in a headlong plunge. But almost as soon as it hit, the force of the impact broke Norman's seat belt and he was hurled to the ground in the wake of the wreckage.

Lufbery ran over to the prostrate Norman, who lay on the ground groaning. He was alive! In the faint light Luf could see that both of Norman's legs were oddly bent. As others ran up to help, Luf shouted, "Don't touch him!"

He leaned over Norman and said gently, "Nimmie, you all right?"

Norman, who could hear other planes above trying to land, gasped out, "Tell them to light some flares. You don't want another fellow to come down and break himself up the way I've done." He was obviously in great pain and had more injuries than the obviously broken legs.

The ambulance finally came and the attendants carefully lifted him into the back. Luf jumped in and the doors slammed shut. The ambulance raced for the hospital at Gérardmer, ten miles away. To ease the pain of the rough ride, Norman held onto Lufbery's powerful hand. As if to cheer up Luf, he sang songs and spoke of what he would do as soon as he had mended and returned to the squadron. Finally, after a long, bumpy, and frightfully painful ride, they arrived at the hospital.

The next day, Thénault, De Laage, and other members of N. 124 and Captain Happe himself came to the hospital. Norman Prince was commissioned a *Sous-Lieutenant* (Second Lieutenant) in the French Air Service and decorated with the Legion of Honor. Happe, the famed fire-eater, softened as he read with great emotion in his voice the citation:

Prince, Norman, Adjutant Pilot of Escadrille N. 124 for nineteen months in escadrille has distinguished himself by a bravery and devotion beyond comparison in the execution of numerous bombardments and pursuit work. Has been grievously wounded the 12 of October, 1916, after having brought down an enemy plane. Already has the Military Medal.

But Norman was unable to hear the words read by the old warrior. He had slipped into a coma that resulted from a blood clot which had formed on his brain. He lay unconscious for two more days and then, on October 15, 1916, Norman Prince died. The man most fully responsible for the founding of the *Escadrille Américaine*, who had loved France almost as much as he had his own America, gave his life to France at the age of twenty-nine.

The Oberndorf mission had been costly. While it disturbed the Germans and caused damage to the Mauser factory, nine bombers had been lost. Captain Happe was sent back to the infantry as a result of the raid, which the High Command did not feel was successful enough. The proof of strategic bombardment would have to wait for a more terrible world war.

The loss of Norman Prince to the *Escadrille Américaine* was a hard blow. His high spirits, his energies and his willingness to challenge the enemy had been an inspiration to all of the Americans. Bert Hall, with typical self-concern, was worried. "So now," he mused, "there are only two of the original seven left—Bill Thaw and myself. Which one of us will go first! I don't think I want to know. Neither does Bill!"

Two days after Norman died orders came through for the squadron to move again. Their special mission—Oberndorf—had been completed and it was time to go back to their regular work. They were to transfer to Cachy, an airdrome on the Somme Front. The big battle had shifted to that sector. It was there that the fate of Bert Hall would be decided.

10 CHANGES AT CACHY

Everything about Cachy was different. Winter had come to France, and the valley of the Somme was a miserable place—cold, damp, muddy and misty. Opened up by heavy English artillery concentrations, the battle had raged since the summer. The battle had originally been planned as a cooperative offensive by the English and French. But, coming as it did after the furnace of Verdun, there were few French divisions left to fight on the

Somme. It was also hoped that the attack along the Somme Front would help take some of the pressure off the French at Verdun.

Once again the war did not go as the great strategists hoped. The Battle of the Somme became the English Verdun. Although early gains were made, they did not amount to much. The heavy guns, which were supposed to clear the way for the advancing English soldiers, filled the battlefield with great craters instead. These shellholes made it difficult for the infantry to move, and made the placement of German machine-gun nests simpler. When the fall rains came, the entire battlefield filled with water holes and became a muddy quagmire. Men literally drowned in the mud.

It was during the Battle of the Somme that the tank was used in war for the first time. But there were too few to have much effect, although on the day they were introduced—September 15, 1916—an allied advance of a mile and a half was made. The lumbering tanks broke down, however, and whatever surprise they might have held for the future was lost.

When the American squadron arrived at Cachy, just south of the Somme River, the winter rains had affected the war on the ground and in the air. The fogs which blew in from the North Sea interfered with flying and the almost constant cold drizzle made life wretched.

After the fine quarters they had enjoyed at their previous stations, their new home was quite a shock to the Americans. Instead of their accustomed villa or hotel they "were directed to a portable barracks newly erected in a sea of mud.

"It was set in a cluster of similar barns nine miles from the nearest town. A sieve was a water-tight compartment in comparison with that elongated shed. The damp cold penetrated through every crack, chilling one to the bone. There were no blankets, and until they were procured, the pilots had to curl up in their flying-clothes. There were no arrangements for cooking and the Americans depended on the other *escadrilles* for food."

There were two combat groups stationed at Cachy, Number

13, to which the American squadron was attached, and Number 12, the famous "Storks"—a total of eight squadrons. Until Bill Thaw returned from Paris with a stove, cooking utensils and other essentials, the men moved from one squadron mess to the other, enjoying the hospitality of their French comrades-in-arms. Their old friend Charles Nungesser was in Esc. N. 65, one of the squadrons in Groupe de Combat 13. The star of the "Storks" was delicate little Georges Guynemer of Esc. N. 3. They were in good company indeed.

They had barely tracked the first gobs of sticky mud into their new hutments when three new men joined them: Frederick Prince, Jr. (Norman's brother), New Yorker Robert Soubiran, an ex-auto racer and mechanic from Minnesota who had served in the Foreign Legion, and Willis B. Haviland from the American Ambulance Field Service. James McConnell—Mac—managed to talk his way out of the hospital to rejoin the squadron for a while. The cold and damp were terrible for his wrenched back, although Mac insisted on flying. He had to be lifted into his Nieuport by two mechanics. But he also spent a good deal of time trying to keep warm in bed. Lufbery, too, was afflicted with rheumatism and in time would have to be sent to the South of France for the warm sunshine there. He did not go, however, before he knocked another German plane out of the hazy skies. The same day, Guynemer, flying a new Spad, the latest French fighter plane, made his twenty-sixth kill.

While at Cachy, perhaps inspired by the numerous "Stork" insignias, the Americans decided they too should have their own personal squadron markings. Each man, if he wished, could have his initials or some other marking painted on his Nieuport, but there had been no uniform squadron identification.

The boxes in which they received ammunition from the Savage Arms Company carried a trademark which bore a rough resemblance to a Seminole Indian chief. Captain Thénault suggested that this would make a fine, very American insignia. All agreed and before long crude though identifiable Indianheads began to appear on the side of the escadrille's Nieuports. Later the Indian was changed to a Sioux chief and the insignias more artistically done. But, however they came out, the Americans were delighted with their own personal markings. The colors were so arranged that from a distance they formed a design in red, white and blue.

This had barely been completed when they had a new problem. In Washington the German ambassador lodged an official complaint with the American government. He called attention to the fact that the newspapers were filled with the exploits of an American escadrille. Certainly this was a violation of American neutrality and, in the name of the German government, Count Bernstorff protested.

Washington communicated with the French Ministry of War, which in time informed Escadrille N. 124 that henceforth "for diplomatic reasons [it] should be called Escadrille des Volontaires, and that [the] name *Escadrille Américaine,* in use at present, must be given up."

To the miserable little band at Cachy, this was ridiculous. Volunteer Squadron? That could mean anybody—they were Americans, and they wanted everyone to know it: the Germans, the French and their own countrymen. Although the new name was official, the Americans refused to use it. It was then that someone, no one now actually knows who, suggested the name *Escadrille Lafayette,* the Lafayette Escadrille. This was a name Kiffin Rockwell, Norman Prince and Victor Chapman would have liked. Dr. Gros liked it too, so much so that he let it be known he had conceived the fittingly romantic name.

So it was that out of the stalemated mire of Cachy the famed whooping-Indian insignia and the name *Lafayette Escadrille* were born.

There remained one final problem: Bert Hall.

The wily little schemer had made himself more and more unpopular with the men of the Lafayette. Without Kiffin to look out for him or to make excuses for him, Bert was not so easily forgiven his small vices. He was, in fact, not a model gentleman. Bert cheated at cards, did not pay his debts, tampered with checks and wrote bad ones. He was always claiming as victories planes no one else saw go down. He was also a ruffian, with a foul tongue and a nasty temper.

He was not very politely asked to leave the squadron. After a few days of this, Bert got the message. He had himself transferred to one of the French squadrons on the field, N. 103, with which he served for about a month. During this period he was credited with another official victory. Bert then requested another transfer to a French aviation mission to Romania. The facts become vague here, for Bert himself never told it the same way twice. Somehow he was granted permission to return to the United States to enlist, as he promised, in the U.S. Air Service. But this never came about; Bert Hall spent the rest of the war as a civilian. He capitalized on his experiences with the Lafayette Escadrille by touring the vaudeville circuits making speeches about himself and the squadron. The French Aviation Service carried Hall on its records as a deserter.

When he left the squadron Bert noted in his diary, "I think the Lafayette Escadrille is glad to get rid of me. I don't blame 'em." It seems to be one of the rare factual statements he ever made. However, in all honesty, Bert Hall had served nearly seven months with the squadron and had not shirked his share of the work. It was his fate, possibly because of a weakness in his character, to be the squadron's non-hero. His departure meant that only two of the original seven members remained: Bill Thaw and McConnell—and Mac was away a great deal in the hospital.

Toward the end of 1916 and the beginning of the next year, when there were few days that the weather was clear enough for patrols, new men were sent to the Lafayette. From the American Ambulance Service came Ronald Hoskier of South Orange,

New Jersey. Hoskier was a slender, handsome young man whose parents were also serving in France. His father was with an ambulance service and his mother in a Paris hospital as a nurse.

On January 25, 1917, one of the squadron's most colorful pilots arrived in the mischievous person of Edwin C. Parsons, "Ted" to his friends. A New Englander who had traveled a good deal, Ted Parsons was a prewar aviator who first served in the American Ambulance Service.

A week before Parsons reported to the squadron he had been preceded by the squadron's youngest member. Tired of waiting around the replacement center, the young aviator just took off and disappeared one day and was listed as a deserter.

This was no new experience for Edmond C. Genêt, who had already "deserted" from the United States Navy to fight for France. He was the baby-faced youth who had listened so avidly at the beginning of the war to Norman Prince on the ship bringing them to France. After spending a year in the Foreign Legion, taking part in many savage battles, Genêt had transferred into aviation. He had a natural love for flying.

"This is what one can call the real thing," he wrote to his mother. "This is sport with all the fascination and excitement and sporting chances any live fellow could ever wish for."

The day Edmond Genêt arrived at Cachy was memorable, and he made quite an impression. As Ted Parsons noted, "Weather conditions were vile, and the ceiling was so low that even the crows were walking." A swirling fog had closed in the field and all patrols for the day were canceled. The men had gathered around the single potbellied stove they had installed in their barracks, hoping to get a little warmth from it.

Suddenly they heard the drone of an engine. It was not a German plane, they could tell from the sound—besides, no German was crazy enough to be out in such weather. One thing was certain, the plane was low, for they could feel the thin walls of the barracks rattling. Forgetting their discomfort for a while, the men waited, listening for the inevitable crash.

Then came the sound of the blipping of the engine, as the pilot turned it off and on as was done when approaching for a landing. Shortly afterward the sound roared up again as the plane taxied in. The fool had managed to land!

The door opened, blowing in a cold blast and fine hard grains of snow, and in came what seemed to be a boy dressed in an aviator's winter suit. He was wrapped in furs and a scarf, with just the tip of his snub red nose showing below his blue eyes. After he had unwrapped the layers and removed his helmet, the men stared in wonder.

"The chunky little figure was topped by a thatch of short-cropped blond hair above the round, innocent, pink-cheeked face of an infant," Ted Parsons wrote. "He didn't look a day over fourteen. His peach-bloom complexion showed no traces of ever having met a razor socially. He had a snubby little nose, and there was a constant expression of pleased surprise at the wonders of the world in the wide-set blue eyes."

He saluted De Laage and Bill Thaw, who were studying him with open-mouthed wonder. In a boyish voice, Genêt informed them that he had just ferried a Nieuport from Plessis-Belleville, the replacement center.

"Good work, Corporal," De Laage answered, "but this is not exactly a day for flying. You might not have arrived, you know."

"It was boring there," Genêt answered. "I was waiting for my orders to come through and when the ceiling lifted a little I decided to fly over."

"Without orders?"

"Yes, but I was due to come soon."

"You are here, so you had better stay," De Laage told him. "I will straighten out your orders." He turned to Soubiran. "Show him his bunk, will you, Bob?"

When Genêt left, De Laage turned to Bill Thaw. "They are now sending us babies. What is this war coming to, Bill?"

Bill chuckled as he read through Edmond Genêt's records. "I'd hate to meet this baby on a battlefield if I were a Boche. Besides, he's twenty."

It took quite a lot of explanation to convince the headquarters at Plessis-Belleville that the man they had listed as a deserter had actually reported for duty with a front-line squadron. Although the others made jokes about this "desertion," Genêt, who was otherwise in good spirits, did not find it amusing.

But of course only he knew that he was also regarded a deserter by the United States Navy.

11 "THIS WAR MAY KILL ME..."

Ten days after Edmond Genêt's dramatic arrival at Cachy, the men were happy to learn that they were to leave the chilly mudhole. They could now boast a full squadron of twelve Americans: Bill Thaw, Charles Chouteau Johnson, Dudley Hill, Didier Masson, Robert Rockwell, Frederick Prince, Jr., Robert Soubiran, Willis Haviland, Ronald Hoskier, Edmond Genêt and Ted Parsons.

About this same time both Mac McConnell and Raoul Lufbery

were away with their respective afflictions—Mac with his back, which made him practically paralyzed, and Luf with rheumatism which forced him to go to Nice for the hot sun. Another casualty was Laurence Rumsey, whose health broke down at Cachy and who was released from the French Air Service and returned to the United States.

Paul Pavelka grew restless with all the inactivity at Cachy and requested a transfer to the Army of the Orient in Macedonia. Always seeking new experiences, Skipper Pavelka had fought many aerial battles but, though he had brought down German planes, was never credited officially. He had even taken off at night from Cachy to attack the German bombers which regularly created havoc at the field. Skipper's pioneering mission nearly ended in disaster, for he neither encountered the German planes nor found the landing field at Cachy. He became lost in the dark and came down many miles from the field. Hoping perhaps to see more conventional action, Skipper jumped at the chance to see another front. Skipper Pavelka was tragically killed on that front when a horse he was riding fell and rolled over on him.

Two days after Pavelka left, the rest of the Lafayette Escadrille moved a few miles south of Cachy to the field at Ravenel near Saint-Just. There were two things immediately in Ravenel's favor, sight unseen: it would be a welcome change after the miseries of Cachy—and it was a few miles closer to Paris.

Upon arrival at the field the men soon learned that they could depend only upon the closer proximity of Paris. If anything, Ravenel was worse than Cachy. There were no barracks at all and for a week they had to sleep on the dirt floors of the underground bomb shelters. The weather was freezing; the wind swept across the empty field with stinging fury. Though he wore three pairs of socks and his fur-lined flying boots, Ted Parsons suffered a frozen toe and was unable to walk for a week.

Edmond Genêt, with customary neatness, dampened his hair one morning with warm wash water. Before he could get a comb through it, it had frozen and he walked around for a while looking as if he had been badly frightened.

To make matters worse—or better, depending upon the point of view—there was little for them to do. Because they were to take part in a big "Spring Offensive," they were told not to expose themselves so that the Germans would not learn that the French were building up their forces in the area. That inactivity only increased boredom and discomfort because the men had more time to think, talk and gripe. On the other hand, it was much colder "upstairs" and flying was almost impossible. Hands, feet and noses froze. Even on clear days it was possible, on a regular patrol, to fly into a snow squall and not only freeze but also get hopelessly lost.

In general, however, there was little activity out of Ravenel. In time, and despite the terrible weather, the French put up a barracks for the Americans. They in turn began to make the great barns as comfortable as possible. They put up partitions so that each man had his own private bunking space. One portion at the end was left open; this served as a kind of clubroom, with the inevitable potbellied stove, a few tables on which books and magazines were piled, a phonograph, and one or two records.

The eager and uncomplaining Edmond Genêt found even these primitive quarters to his liking. Possibly in the back of his mind, too, he knew he was safe from the arm of the United States Navy's police and the Department of Justice. That he had run away from the comfort and safety of the Navy into the danger and miseries of wartime France would have made little difference to the officials.

It's a big relief to me to be out here at last, dear mother [Genêt wrote]. *The rumble of the big guns this morning which roused me from beneath my warm covering of four big blankets (for it's right cold here and we've snow all over the ground) wasn't new music to my ears. It seemed like old times, the roar of old comrades . . . .*

Our living room, where we are most of the time when off duty, is a mighty attractive little den. We have covered all the walls and ceiling with corrugated cardboard strips (smooth side outside) over the rough boards, and on this in various places I have drawn and painted vivid scenes of aerial combats between French and German machines. We have a huge painting of an Indian head, the symbol of the escadrille, *which is also painted on each of our machines. The Indian's mouth is open as though he was shouting his terrible war-cry in defiance of his enemies, and he looks very warlike indeed. It's quite an appropriate symbol for the* escadrille, *being something genuinely American.*

Genêt's greatest thrills came from the rare patrols they were able to fly out of Ravenel. On one of them, led by the ever-reliable Bill Thaw, Genêt's friend Ted Parsons found himself in a good deal of trouble. It was one of his first patrols and might easily have been his last, except for luck and skill: luck on his part and skill on the part of a mysterious intruder.

"Fresh from that long intensive course of training in the schools," Parsons later recalled, "I felt there wasn't much I didn't know about pursuit and combat work. I had been told I was pretty hot stuff by my instructors, who made it legal by signing their names to high recommendations in my flight book."

About a half-dozen Nieuports with the whooping Indianhead on their sides took off in the chill of the morning and headed out for a patrol of the lines. For an hour they froze and flew. "It got most monotonous," Ted Parsons said, "particularly for a man so full of desire to clean up the front single-handed."

With thrilling unexpectedness Ted saw five moving specks down low, inside the German lines. How he swelled with pride; while the others were burning up the gas and joyriding, he had found the hated Hun. What he didn't know was that Bill Thaw had seen the five German planes long before, not to mention others Ted had not seen at all. Bill's orders were to keep the lines clear of German planes. The ones they saw were too far inside the lines to do the French any harm.

But Ted Parsons could not accept that. He jammed on full throttle and dived past Bill, waggling his wings as he went by. As he did, he also pointed wildly at the German planes. He was rather put out to catch a fleeting glimpse of Bill shaking his head negatively.

Hoping that the rest of the patrol was following, Ted plunged into the fray. As he passed over the lines German antiaircraft guns, "Archie," as antiaircraft fire was called by the men, opened up on him. The bursts went wide of the mark and gave Ted "a momentary thrill." This was really it! With intrepid confidence he warmed up his gun on the way to battle.

The five German ships grew larger as Ted charged down upon them. They were in a fine formation—two-seaters they were; practically sitting ducks. His courage exceeding his battle wisdom, Ted Parsons started his gun chattering a half-mile away from the German formation. If they had not already seen him, his premature firing would have alerted them. Almost instantly the five planes scattered as Ted arrived to dive through the formation.

He hadn't hit a thing. In addition, no one else in the escadrille had followed him. He soon became the center of attention as the five two-seaters converged on him and began firing. "The attack was coming from every side," Ted could see. "Blue ravelings from tracer bullets crisscrossed the sky."

The intrepid airman was suddenly transformed into "a very scared youth." Kicking his Nieuport into a steep bank and giving it full throttle, Ted pulled out of the death trap and raced for the French lines. As if nothing had occurred, the five German planes reformed and flew on.

Still frightened, Ted looked back over his shoulder for any other German planes. The trenches seemed miles away. The German Archie opened up again, indicating that a French plane was overhead. Even if it rarely hit a plane, Archie was always a signal to its own pilots, just as the French antiaircraft bursts were to French pilots. German bursts were usually black and French white, so that respective pilots would have little trouble in reading the signals.

Ted was so anxious to get away from the danger behind him that he did not keep his eyes on the sky ahead. He had almost reached the lines when a number of dark shadows passed before his eyes. Something was in the sun. He looked up and saw three more two-seaters, ones he had not seen before. Certain he could not escape twice, Ted merely tightened up inside the cockpit and waited for the impact of the bullets.

Nothing happened. Surprised, Ted worked up enough courage to glance upward. The three planes were on the run for their lines. Chasing them was a single Nieuport with an Indianhead painted on the side. The pilot was handling the plane like a virtuoso. He seemed to be all over the sky, dancing around the three planes, his gun stitching across their wings, into the fuselages. He must have already hit two of the rear gunners, for only one seemed to be firing back.

Though low on gas, Ted watched the performance with awe. He had never seen such skilled air fighting. He reluctantly turned again toward the lines and watched the battle over his shoulder. He wondered, too, who of the patrol had decided to save his skin.

As he watched, one of the two-seaters burst into flame. Belching smoke, it fell, twisting and burning, into the German lines. The remaining two German planes had reached the safety of their own lines with dead or wounded aboard.

Flying through the puffs of Archie, the lone Nieuport caught up with Ted just over friendly lines. Together they returned to the field and landed almost simultaneously. Still shaking, Ted managed to crawl out of the cockpit. Unsteadily he made his way over to the other plane to thank the other pilot. "He raised his goggles and looked me over as he would a strange bug," Ted wrote later. "It was Lufbery." Having returned from the South of France, Luf had learned that a patrol was out. His rheumatism having been cured somewhat, he jumped into his Nieuport and had arrived just in time to rescue Ted Parsons, former intrepid Hun-hunter, and to be credited with his seventh official victory.

Lufbery then proceeded to haul Ted over the coals, beginning with "Well, what a dumb fool you are . . ." and taking off from there. Having done that, he advised Ted on the foolishness of lone patrols (which, of course, was what Lufbery himself had done) and then congratulated him for his courage. It was foolhardy, but it was courage. The kind, Luf warned, which could get him killed—as it did so many green pilots.

"But," Luf said smiling, "you show good spirit. I think you need a drink. Let's go."

McConnell also rejoined the Lafayette Escadrille at Saint-Just. Mac could not remain in the hospital while the rest fought. That he was in constant misery did not seem to matter to him. Nor did he realize the seriousness of his injury, complicated by rheumatism. Though he could walk better than before, the paralysis had gotten to Mac's neck. This meant that he was unable to turn his head from side to side or raise it. These movements were essential to a fighter pilot, whose neck, for all practical purposes, should have been set on a swivel. Despite this, Mac insisted upon taking part in patrols.

He had flown into the field on March 12, 1917; two days later he would be thirty years old, old for a fighter pilot. Mac was, like so many in the squadron, devoted to their cause.

"This war may kill me," Mac wrote on the last day of his twenty-ninth year, "but I have it to thank for much." He neglected to explain what it was he owed the war, but he had found good companionship. His life, which had seemed to be drifting two years before, now had a purpose and direction. Mac was involved in a great adventure and he knew he was on the side of the right, that he was fighting for justice. It bothered him that he had to spend so much time being treated for a sore back.

Of the first four men who had reported to Captain Thénault back in April 1916, only he was still alive. Kiffin, Victor and Norman had all "gone west." Mac wanted to do his part as well as avenge the death of his friends.

One week after his return to the squadron, Mac took off on a patrol in the company of Edmond Genêt and Ted Parsons. It was a gray day—March 19, 1917—when they took off on the ten-o'clock patrol. They were barely airborne when Parsons had trouble. An oil line clogged, a common thing those cold days, and his rotary engine ground to a stop. Trailing smoke, he had to land in the nearest open field.

Mac and Genêt continued on into the clouded sky toward the lines. On one side of them, to the left, they saw the Somme making a wide irregular curve and then running past the city of Ham, which was still held by the Germans. On the other side, to their right, ran the Oise River. They were just east of Ham when they passed into German territory. When they flew toward Saint-Quentin Mac and Genêt spied two German two-seaters. The two enemy planes were headed toward French lines, probably on a reconnaissance mission. After exchanging signals, wing-waggling and waving their arms, Mac and Genêt moved up for the attack.

The two Nieuports climbed to get above the enemy machines. They were soon in the clouds, with Mac in the lead. "I mounted to attack the nearest and left Mac to take care of the second," Genêt wrote. "There were plenty of clouds and mist, and after I had finished my scrap, in which I got one of my main upper-wing supports cut in half, a guiding-rod cut in half, several bullets through my upper wing, and half an explosive bullet in my left cheek, which stunned me for a moment, I went down to look for Mac and help him if he was hard-pressed."

But there was no other plane in sight. Genêt, his face bleeding and painful, circled the area searching for a sign of Mac. He remained there for fifteen minutes, despite his wounds and the fact that his wing might snap in two at any moment. Finally he knew he had to return to the field. Maybe Mac had already returned.

Genêt flew low almost all of the way home, searching the

ground for a sight of Mac's plane. He saw nothing but the burned villages and destroyed fields of France, churned up by shellfire and distorted by winter winds and frost.

Mac's plane had not returned to Saint-Just. Neither did he return during the rest of the day nor was there any word of him: no one had seen him land or fall, nor had he landed at any of their other airfields. Mac had simply disappeared. Genêt had his wounds treated and was obviously badly upset over the disappearance of Mac. As seemed the custom with wounded men of the Lafayette, Genêt refused to go to a hospital to get the painful cuts on his face treated. He became dispirited, solitary and gloomy—all unusual for him.

When they found Mac's last note, addressed to the squadron, Edmond Genêt almost went to pieces. It was a note typical of Mac (who was a full ten years older than Edmond): "My burial is of no import," it read in part. "Make it as easy as possible on yourselves. I . . . do not care for any service. If the omission would embarrass you, I presume I could stand the performance."

Three days later during a French infantry advance, the *poilus* overran the small village of Flavy-le-Martel, where they found a Nieuport which had struck with great impact. Its engine was deeply buried in the earth and the rest of the plane had been reduced almost to matchsticks by the force of its crash. Beside it lay the body of the pilot—the Germans had stripped him of everything—clothes, shoes, wristwatch, ring, money—even his identification papers. Only when they found the plane's number, still readable on the rudder, could they identify the pilot. The number was 2055; the plane was Mac's.

The news arrived by field phone, as all squadrons were informed of the newly found wreck. De Laage hurried to the barracks, threw the door open and stood in the doorway. As Parsons wrote, "He stood there, silent, with a godawful expression of unbearable sorrow and pain on his face."

Finally De Laage managed to speak.

"They have found him," he said. "Jim is dead . . . one of the best . . ."

Unable to finish, De Laage quickly turned and left. The other men stopped the game they had been playing, went to their separate rooms and remained there for the rest of the afternoon.

Genêt brooded over Mac's death, feeling for some reason responsible. He could not understand that Mac's physical condition, the fact that he could not turn his head to keep an eye on all directions at once, all but doomed him. While Mac had been busy with the plane he had attacked, either another two-seater or the one which had shot up Genêt got behind and caught him dead in his sights. Mac never had a chance and was killed instantly by a fusillade of machine-gun fire. He had had no opportunity to turn off the engine, which raced out of control in the death dive.

This fact made little impression upon the "poor little dreamer," as Ted Parsons so fittingly called Edmond Genêt. He burned with a hatred for the Germans as he had never before.

"My blood boils and thirsts after those accursed Huns. They're brutes and fiends and daily they grow worse. I'll get a Boche yet, or more than one, to avenge poor Mac." Genêt was ignoring Mac's advice and was not making it easy on himself. The other men warned him almost daily not to take so many chances or to be so reckless. But the little dreamer would not listen.

He was not elated as were the others when they learned that on April 6, 1917, the United States had declared war upon Germany. During March the English and French were making advances as they had not done in years. To keep up with the advance the squadron was moved from Ravenel up to Ham, a few miles from where Mac had fallen. Big things were happening in 1917. There was much talk about a great offensive to be mounted by France's General Robert Nivelle which—the General promised —would swiftly end the war. What he, the English and the Americans did not know was that the Germans had been, through most of March, pulling back to strong positions along what would come to be called the Hindenburg Line.

Behind them the Germans left a desolation of poisoned wells, ruined fruit trees and farms: a wasteland they were happy to give to the English and French. At the Hindenburg Line the Germans set up their deadly machine-gun nests which made the Western Front one vast death trap. It was into this that Nivelle launched his offensive, the Second Battle of the Aisne.

Nivelle's offensive opened on April 16, 1917. The guns boomed all along the front as a terrible prelude: eleven million shells along a fifty-mile-wide sector. By the second day it was obvious that Nivelle had not kept and would not keep his promise: the war would not end that day, or that year. Once again the *poilus* were slaughtered; nearly a generation was wiped out in the foolish thrust. It was after this battle and the loss of 120,000 men that Nivelle was relieved and there was a serious mutiny in the French Army. Entire divisions refused to respond to orders and those that did would march to the Front *baa*ing like sheep being led to slaughter.

On the morning that Nivelle's ill-fated and at the same time impressive offensive began, Genêt and one of the newer pilots, Walter Lovell, took off on the early-morning patrol. It was nearly a month since Mac had been killed, but Genêt had not recovered. If anything he had grown worse; he looked ill, tired and nervous. The men did not know that, besides brooding over Mac's death, young Genêt had something else on his mind. Late in March he had learned from his mother that a girl he had hoped to marry had become engaged to someone else. This only increased Edmond's reckless behavior on patrols.

When he and Lovell returned from the morning patrol, which had been uneventful except for the broiling shellfire on the ground, Genêt became angry when someone mentioned that he did not look well.

"You should lay off for a while," Lovell suggested.

"No!" Genêt snapped back and walked away.

When Lufbery and Willis Haviland were about to leave on the 2:30 P.M. patrol, it was learned that Haviland's Nieuport had developed engine trouble. Haviland then tried to borrow Genêt's plane and was refused. Instead, the fatigued Genêt climbed into the plane himself and followed Lufbery.

Because of the low cloud ceiling they had to fly lower than normally and attracted a good deal of Archie fire. They were up around 5000 feet when the black bursts became especially persistent. Luf turned around and saw Genêt's Nieuport practically in the center of a series of bursts. The youngster immediately turned and seemed to head back for home. Luf turned to follow and then, satisfied that Genêt was flying all right, turned back to flying the patrol alone.

Below, the French infantrymen watched the little plane make a sudden turn and then plummet down in a tight wing-wracking spin. One wing pulled off as the plane howled down at more than 200 miles an hour into a hard-surfaced road. Edmond Genêt fell only a few hundred meters from the spot where Mac had fallen.

Genêt, officially listed as a deserter from a United States Navy that had not yet fired a shot in the war, was the first American citizen to die in battle after the American declaration of war. After the war his name was cleared by Secretary of the Navy Josephus Daniels. Thus in death was the burden lifted, for it had weighed heavily in life upon the twenty-year-old Edmond Genêt.

It seemed that the Lafayette was suffering a run of bad luck at this time. Some pilots blamed the bad luck on a mongrel dog called Archie; others blamed it on Monday. It seemed that there were a string of fatal encounters on Mondays—both Mac and Genêt had died on Mondays.

The dog Archie had belonged to Genêt and was then adopted by Ronald Hoskier. One Monday Hoskier decided to take a turn over the lines in a two-seater Morane Parasol. It was a slow plane and was so named because its fuselage seemed to hang below the single upper wing as if dangling from a parasol. The squadron was being re-equipped with the new, tough Spads at this time and the Parasol was scheduled to be retired. Hoskier wanted to give it a flight before that happened. He took along with him Jean Dressy, De Laage's orderly and a good gunner.

Reluctantly Thénault granted the two men permission to go over the lines on Monday, April twenty-third. Over the lines they were attacked by three Albatros fighters. These were the latest of the new German planes, fast, maneuverable and deadly. The Morane was no match for a single Albatros, let alone three. The slow French plane was far behind the Nieuports and Spads of the other Lafayette men when the Albatroses sliced out of the clouds and, within minutes, shot the wing off the Morane. Hoskier and Dressy had put up a good fight but were outmatched and, still inside the wingless fuselage, rocketed into the ground.

At the double funeral two days later, Hoskier's parents came from their own war posts to attend the services. De Laage was terribly affected by the death of Dressy, whose family had been employed by De Laage's for years. Jean Dressy, in the early weeks of the war, had pulled the wounded De Laage from the battlefield to safety.

Possibly as a gesture to his friend Hoskier as well as to Dressy, Alfred de Laage de Meux took the friendless jinx-hound Archie in. Three weeks after the death of Hoskier and Dressy—on a Monday—De Laage had the opportunity to fly an old warplane he had never flown before, an old Morane-Saulnier "Bullet." This single-wing plane, one of the first to be used with a primitive device for shooting forward through the propeller arc, looked like a distant ancestor of the new Spads and Nieuports on the field at Ham. It was a tricky plane to fly and for even so expert a pilot as De Laage it was a challenge.

His takeoff was his usual dashing exhibition of skill and cool nerve. He raced the engine up, signaled for the wheel chocks to be pulled and raced down the field. The Bullet lifted off the ground and, as was his custom, De Laage pulled back on the stick to zoom away in one of his steep climbing turns. This was a dangerous practice, for a plane had barely reached flying speed at this point, but for a pilot of De Laage's ability it was nothing special.

The Morane Bullet was barely a hundred feet off the ground

when the Le Rhône engine quit. The plane stopped, turned on one wing and dropped heavily to the ground. When De Laage was extricated from the tangled wreckage he was already dead. Instead of dying in battle, as had many of his illustrious ancestors, the likable De Laage perished in an unnecessary accident—one of the ironic tragedies of war. As a patrol leader De Laage had distinguished himself fearlessly; he had three official victories with the Lafayette Escadrille.

His most spectacular victory had occurred shortly after Mac's death during a period when the squadron was plagued by a series of accidents which put one plane after another out of service. Taking off alone, De Laage had zoomed off toward the Front, where he spotted a single French plane beset by four German fighters. Swooping into the battle De Laage shot down two of the attacking Germans, thus saving not only the French plane but also a nearby observation balloon the Germans were trying to burn. This unusual double victory was quickly confirmed and De Laage was made a Chevalier of the Legion of Honor for his exploit.

His loss to the Lafayette Escadrille, as its second-in-command, a role he often shared with Bill Thaw, was a bad blow. Morale was low: would there be no end to the killing? Would there ever be an end to the war?

12 THE LAST KNIGHTS

With the United States finally in the war it would only be a matter of time. A few weeks, perhaps; at most a month or three and
the war would be over. After the Nivelle offensive the French
were all but exhausted. So were the English. There only remained the Flanders campaign before they too would have sac-
rificed their men in battles that seemed to decide nothing. Meanwhile the Germans, still in France after three years of war, waited

in their so-called Hindenburg Line. This was, in effect, like some monstrous sponge which absorbed human life, French, British—and German.

With the coming of the Americans, fresh young blood, all would be changed. The old European powers were tired; the men of the New World, young, brash, daring, spoiling for a go at the Hun, would turn the tide.

American leaders unfortunately promised more than they could deliver. Although war had been declared in April 1917, and the first troops arrived in France in June, it would be October before they would be ready for battle. A good deal could happen in six months, and the Germans hurriedly planned their Big Offensive before the Americans arrived.

As for aviation, the United States Aircraft Production Board rashly promised "regiments and brigades of winged cavalry mounted on gas-driven flying horses" which would "sweep the Germans from the sky."

Gearing a nation for war after decades of avoiding foreign entanglements proved to be anything but simple or speedy. The very words of the Aircraft Production Board (which consisted mainly of automobile manufacturers) gave their good intentions away. They still were in the era of the horse and the cavalry and had little understanding of the airplane as a war machine. Nor did the newly organized American Air Service, a branch of the Signal Corps. When war came to the United States there was not one airworthy battleplane in the entire country. While the European aircraft made great strides in design and in engines, America—the home of the first successful aircraft—lagged behind. Despite the promises, made no doubt honestly but unwisely, it would be a full year before the American Air Service would get into battle—and not one American-made plane would darken the skies over Germany.

For that long period between the American declaration of war and the first American-German aerial combats, only the Lafayette Escadrille would serve as representatives of their country's air

illiam Thaw, center, talks to French pilots who have shot down a German two-seater.

fighters. They too one day would be transferred to the American Air Service; it was something to look forward to with excitement.

Meanwhile, the Great War dragged on and there were patrols to fly. Flying out of Ham and taking part in the Battle of the Aisne was a grim business. This was underscored by the loss in too swift succession of Mac, Genêt, Hoskier and Dressy. De Laage's death, more tragic because it had not occurred in battle, brought home the risk of flying.

During this period Bill Thaw distinguished himself for patrol work, some flights adding up to ten hours in the air in a single day. Working down dangerously low and in close contact with the French, Bill furnished reliable and valuable information on the retreat of the Germans.

The Lafayette Escadrille was undoubtedly the most famous unit in France, possibly in the world. Both the French and the Germans encouraged widespread publicity for their air heroes, which they found good for civilian morale. With men dying by the thousands every day in the trenches, the exploits of the intrepid airmen, the Knights of the Air as they were often called, were read avidly by the people back home. The stories took their minds off the mass slaughter and concentrated attention on romantic young heroes.

The English did not choose to publicize individuals or any single branch of the service, feeling that it would be bad for the morale of the troops. Even so, the names of their own Aces (a term generally not encouraged by the British), Albert Ball, Edward Mannock, William Bishop (a Canadian) and James McCudden among others, began to appear in the newspapers.

Germany had its own national hero in The Red Knight, the chilling killer Ace, Manfred von Richthofen. He was the honor student of that avid teacher Oswald Boelcke, one of Germany's first air heroes and the major German air fighter to face the American squadron at Verdun in 1916. Boelcke died after a collision in the air with another of his students.

Like the French Aces Guynemer, Nungesser and René Fonck,

...rles Nungesser in his Nieuport, which carried his personal insignia.

the members of the Lafayette Escadrille enjoyed wide celebrity. Their adventures were exaggerated, to their embarrassment, in the papers back home and then sent around the world. Up to the time of the United States' entry into the war only Lufbery was an Ace with nine confirmed victories to his credit. He, like many others, had accounted for many more German planes, but without the proper ground witnesses they were not official.

The fame of the escadrille attracted more enlistments during the final months before America's entry into the war.

Thus did the roster of the Lafayette grow. By 1917 there were so many Americans in French flying schools that not all graduates could be sent to the Lafayette Escadrille; some were stationed with other French squadrons. These men, many of whom never served with Escadrille N. 124, were members of the Lafayette Flying Corps, Dr. Gros' own elaboration on Norman Prince's original idea. In all, a total of thirty-eight Americans served with the Lafayette Escadrille; in addition, nearly 200 other men served in the Lafayette Flying Corps, either in French squadrons or in American squadrons.

This has led to a great deal of confusion and many claims by men (or their families) who had not actually served with the Lafayette Escadrille. Many Americans who never had been members of the original Lafayette Escadrille nonetheless distinguished themselves. Among these were Frank Baylies, Thomas Hitchcock, Jr., Jean Huffer, David E. Putnam, William A. Wellman (famous after the war as a movie director), Benjamin Walcott and dozens of others.

But the uniqueness of the Lafayette Escadrille is a carefully tended quality. It set them apart because, for whatever the personal reasons, these thirty-eight men were among the first to recognize the threat of Germany's war to their own country or even, in a wider sense, to civilization. They were a group of men set apart from all the others, however courageous and effective as warriors in the air, because they were the first.

That they were exploited by the French as propaganda material by no means detracts from the motives of the men themselves. However cynical and wasteful of human life the old generals had become, there still remained idealists who believed in a cause. In 1917, however, the cause had shifted somewhat. It was no longer so much a hatred of an enemy who threatened civilization as it was a growing realization that war itself was the enemy. They were all trapped by this common enemy—the Germans, the French, the British and now the Americans, all locked in battle without point and without end.

Ray Bridgman, one of the new men, was a sensitive idealist who was also a realist. Though one of the finest pilots of the Lafayette, whose Spad was one of the most battle-scarred, this young man from Lake Forest, Illinois, looked upon the war as anything but adventure. Riding in a train through the French countryside one spring day he wrote, "The joy and thrill of the spring enhances the poignancy of the plight of Europe. How long must the slaughter continue! Grim and unutterable loss fills all the human atmosphere, though the flowers nod as gayly and the songs of the birds are as sweet as though the world were singing through the Infinite, as it might, instead of being a chaos of mud and death." And some weeks later he would say, "A royal sunset crowned the beauty of this summer day. Now, in the night, a great clean wind is sweeping up across France, Spain, Italy, the Mediterranean. One is glad to breathe deep of its power. Northward it sweeps across the graves of unnumbered thousands of Europe's youth.

"Their spirits do not rouse me to hatred. They are from both sides and all are youth—and they believed."

Other fine young men came to the Lafayette around this time: Stephen Bigelow, Walter Lovell, Harold B. Willis (all from Massachusetts); Edward Hinkle (who was over forty when he joined the squadron); Thomas Hewitt, Jr., Kenneth Marr, John A. Drexel. Drexel was an aristocrat and an outstanding aviator from Philadelphia who took his position in society a bit too seriously.

Hewitt was a special case. He had come from the comforts of a good home in Westchester, New York. He served for a while in the Ambulance Service and then switched to aviation. He proved himself a good pilot in flying school, did well in gunnery and acrobatics. His record impressed Bill Thaw and De Laage on one of their tours of the French flying schools in search of good men for the escadrille. Once at the Front, however, Hewitt soon earned the nickname "Horrible." He had lost his taste for battle somewhere along the line from the replacement pool to the airfield.

He seemed unable to do anything right. The situation came to a head one day when the squadron moved from the field at Ham to a new one at Chaudun. Those who had planes would fly them, and while the field was a good-sized one, it had one obstacle the men were warned to look out for. An irrigation ditch ran across one end. This was clearly marked with flags and was not a serious obstacle.

It was to Hewitt. Flying one of the new Spads, he was the last to come in. All other pilots had landed and pulled out of the way. Hewitt seemed to have trouble making up his mind where he would land. Then he bounced down, rolled toward the far boundary of the field.

"The ditch, the ditch!" the others yelled, but it made no difference. Poor "Horrible" went directly into the ditch at high speed. It was ten feet wide, which gave him plenty of room in which to smash the Spad up into a useless wreck.

Captain Thénault, in one of his rare moods of extreme anger, tore into Hewitt. He then proceeded to make his own big mistake of the day. As punishment he ordered Hewitt to drive back to Ham, where he was to pick up Robert Soubiran's Spad and bring it to Chaudun. Soubiran was then on a short leave. Thénault reasoned that the long bumpy ride would jolt some sense into Hewitt.

Night had fallen and the delivery would have to wait till morning. Thénault and the others were out on the line the next day to observe the arrival of Soubiran's Spad.

Before long they heard and then saw the powerful fighter plane approaching the field. As they watched, Hewitt brought

the plane down, touched the ground and then proceeded to put Soubiran's new Spad in the ditch.

This was more than the Captain could bear, and he quickly grounded Hewitt, who in time left the squadron and was released by the French as unfit for flying duty.

Another noteworthy personality was Andrew Courtney Campbell, Jr., of Chicago. Gifted (although many would have argued that point, insisting that *cursed* would be the better word) with an irrepressible sense of fun, Campbell was constantly stirring up trouble—it didn't matter to him whether on the ground or in the air.

Campbell was a dashing type, complete with dapper mustache, snappy uniform and a casual air. After a particularly trying day, when the men were hoping for a quiet dinner, Campbell would burst out with a loud, old and bad joke. If no one laughed, he would try again. His efforts at humor were generally greeted with a request, the wording of which ran something to the effect of: "Curse you, Campbell! Shut up, will you?"

But such appeals had little effect. Neither did threats of violence ("Campbell, if you do that again I'm going to give you a bust in the nose"). One of his chief delights was closing in on

Chaudun, July 1917. The new Spads may be seen along with a single Nieuport. Kenneth Marr is walking on the left.

Courtesy Paul A. Rockwell

someone in the air just to see how close he could come. "He was a pain in the neck on patrols," Ted Parsons recalled, "particularly to the man directly in front of him. Many times, when I had been leading a patrol, I came back with the leaping jitters if he had been behind me, for he'd keep his whirling propeller blades not three feet from my tail. I'd spend more time trying to keep out of his way than I would looking for Boches."

Campbell was a superb, if slightly crazy, pilot. But his behavior invited accidents. One day at Chaudun he took off in a Nieuport to see what it could do—and to show what he could do. Over the field Campbell threw the fighter through a harrowing series of acrobatics. With singing wires and quivering wings the Nieuport rolled, zoomed and dived—this last to send the spectators running for cover.

Thoroughly enjoying himself, Campbell would pull up in a climb. He would then snap over into a loop and dive again. Laughing, no doubt intrepidly, Campbell would pull up again. On one of these climbs he had just reached the top of the loop, and was hanging upside down in the cockpit when he heard a loud twanging and a crack!

Twisting his head to the left and looking up at the brilliant blue sky, Campbell saw that the entire lower left wing had snapped off his plane. It was an interesting problem, for he was up well over 5000 feet with only two-thirds of his wings. As the wing panel fluttered to the ground the men below prepared for the next act in the drama. They sent for what they called the "meat wagon," for Campbell's luck had really run out. The Nieuport would have to spin in, lose another wing or two and end his career as a flying jester.

Righting the Nieuport, Campbell very carefully put it into a slow glide. He realized that if he tried to spiral into the field below, the strain would snap the other wings. Holding the plane in precarious balance, he kept it in a straight, flat glide. He sighted what appeared to be a smooth field about six miles away.

Lafayette Spad, suffering engine failure, crashes into a headquarters building.

As he guided his crippled Nieuport a large object tumbled by: the now-useless wing.

When the meat wagon pulled into a beetfield they found, instead of a messy crash, the cool Campbell calmly smoking a cigarette and studying the three-winged Nieuport. The panel had come off neatly at the root, leaving dangling wires and even the V strut between the upper and lower wings. Great skill—and even more luck—had pulled Campbell through again. Within half an hour he was in the air again.

Shortly after Campbell arrived, a French replacement for the beloved Alfred de Laage de Meux arrived in the person of Antoine Arnoux de Maison-Rouge. A former cavalry officer, Maison-Rouge found himself in a difficult position. He had proved himself, had even been cited, while serving with another French escadrille. But the Americans had been genuinely fond of De Laage and found it difficult to warm up to another second-in-command. Maison-Rouge had a further difficulty in that he did not understand the Americans as De Laage had. Maison-Rouge found them, often rightly, undisciplined and not very military.

It only took Campbell to prove Maison-Rouge more than correct.

Maison-Rouge one day led a patrol consisting of Campbell, Bridgman, David Peterson, a new pilot, Kenneth Marr and "good old" Campbell. They tangled with a German formation of Albatroses and Peterson came out of the battle with his first official victory. The six Lafayette Escadrille pilots then headed back for home with Maison-Rouge in the lead. Unfortunately for him, he was followed by Campbell.

All the way from the lines the wheels of Campbell's Spad dangled close above Maison-Rouge's head. The Frenchman shouted and waved at Campbell but, as usual, it had no effect. Looking up, Maison-Rouge could see Campbell's smiling face with terrible clarity. He could also see the wheels of Campbell's Spad dancing over his head and all but skimming his own upper wing.

They had come in over the field when Campbell became even more frisky. His Spad was almost directly over Maison-Rouge's, and he lifted his plane up and down in what he must have thought a joyful manner. On one of the bounces, either he misjudged or Maison-Rouge's plane bounced up at the same moment Campbell's dropped down.

What happened next could only have happened to Campbell: the wheels of his Spad broke through the surface of the top wing of Maison-Rouge's plane—and the two planes fastened together. Once again the meat wagon was at the ready.

Thus locked together, the tandem Spads completed two turns over the field as the pilots tried to decide what to do next. Maison-Rouge was certain what his fate would be; they were bound to crash. No one could tell what Campbell was thinking.

On the second turn, Campbell suddenly pushed the throttle and pulled back on the stick. The two planes came apart, leaving Maison-Rouge with a badly damaged wing. Expecting to lose it any minute, he gently nursed the Spad down and landed safely.

Campbell went on to entertain all, except the by-now quite sick Maison-Rouge, with a further exhibition of his prowess. He stunted the Spad in a hair-raising demonstration before setting it down for a perfect landing. When he made it obvious that he should be congratulated for the manner in which he had handled the emergency (forgetting conveniently that he had caused it), his compatriots began to wonder which side Campbell was on.

Shortly thereafter, Maison-Rouge's health broke and he requested a transfer out of the Lafayette Escadrille. Once again, Courtney Campbell had eluded fate: not only had his Spad escaped damage, Campbell himself got off with little more than a scolding from the Captain.

Among the new arrivals was another man who was afflicted with luck. It could not, with any accuracy, be called either good or bad; *strange* would be the better description. The man was James Norman Hall, a writer from Colfax, Iowa. He was not related to the infamous Bert. Jimmy Hall had spent about half a year in the trenches with the Royal Fusiliers (though how he managed to enlist in a British outfit without taking the usual oath of allegiance is unknown) in 1915. Hall survived some of the worst fighting of the early months of the war and then returned to America.

Planning to return to France to do some articles on the Lafayette Escadrille, Jimmy ended up not only doing the articles but also enlisting in the squadron. Though he was just about thirty, considered ancient for a fighter pilot, Jimmy proved a proficient pilot and joined the escadrille at Chaudun.

On one of his first patrols with Spa. 124 (as the escadrille was designated because it was now outfitted mainly with Spads), Hall distinguished himself with a most unusual incident. He was "sky man" (he took a patrol position high above the others to cover them from an attack from above); Ted Parsons was the leader and William Dugan and Walter Lovell comprised the rest of the patrol. They flew above the bloody Chemin-des-Dames, now in

French hands. Although they were under Archie fire, they flew for an hour without seeing any German planes. Parsons led the patrol a short distance inside the German lines.

Unexpectedly three enemy two-seaters appeared below them. Waggling his wings, Parsons signaled Lovell and Dugan and, with Hall as top cover, each selected one of the German planes for attack. They whipped down in screaming dives, rasped off a few rounds of machine-gun bullets and pulled away. The Germans dodged and returned the fire.

No results.

Turning, the three Spads again made an attempt, only to find themselves under withering fire from the two-seaters. Then they tried to gang up on a single plane, attacking from below. "That didn't work so well either," Parsons has written, "for while we were after him his pals were raking us from each side, and it began to look like a rough stand-off."

Parsons was baffled. There seemed to be no way to get at the two-seaters effectively. Still, even if they couldn't knock planes out of the sky, at least they could keep them on their own side of the lines.

Studying the situation, he chanced to look up and saw a single Spad streaking down upon the last of the German planes. It was slightly away from the other two, making it a good isolated target. Of course, Parsons thought, good old Jimmy Hall. He had almost forgotten about him above the fight. Now, with the German's attention held by the other three Spads, Jimmy would swoop down and pop one off.

But the German observer also spotted Hall's zooming plane. Turning his Spandau machine guns around, he began peppering away at the Spad. Parsons marveled at Hall's cool nerve. He was plunging directly into the German machine-gun fire and he still held his own. The Spad was a powerful ship and it could, unlike the Nieuport (and most German planes), be pulled out of a near-vertical dive and still keep its wings on.

Despite this, Parsons was worried. Hall continued "sizzling through the air, and still no sign of firing."

If his guns were jammed, Hall could have pulled away to get out of the steady stream of fire from the German plane's rear cockpit. There could be no other end to it now: the two planes would collide. Perhaps Jimmy had been hit already. The German gunner saw it coming, himself. He dropped his guns and ducked inside the cockpit.

The Spad's wheels and wingtip brushed against the top wing of the German plane. The Spad then rolled over and began a dizzying spin. The enemy two-seater righted itself and pulled for home. Parsons watched Jimmy Hall's plane spinning to the ground.

On completing the patrol Parsons led Lovell and Dugan back to the field with misgivings. He would have to report "that poor old Jim had finally gotten it."

After he pulled himself out of the Spad, Parsons turned to be greeted by none other than "poor old Jim."

After showing how happy he was to see Jim, Ted Parsons demanded to know what happened. With a touch of embarrassment on his handsome face, Hall related what had happened. He had indeed collided with the German plane and after he fell into the spin was certain his number had come up. But the sturdy plane, with a bent wingtip and a broken wing rib, responded to his desperate hand on the controls. But not before Jim Hall spun down for 6000 feet, wondering all the way what would happen. When he pulled out of the spin he turned for home and found on landing that his wing was cracked and that there were a few bullet-holes in the plane. Otherwise, there was no serious damage to man or plane.

Parsons listened, gratified that Jimmy's luck had held. But he sensed there was more.

"But what happened in the dive?" he asked. "Did your gun jam?"

Jimmy's face turned crimson. He looked around to see if anyone else was about.

"I was so busy getting the German plane in my sights . . ."

He paused, looked around again.

"Yes," Ted prodded him.

". . . that I forgot to pull the trigger!"

Parsons had no comment for that confession.

There was one other classic incident. This one occurred shortly after Jimmy's arrival at the squadron field. As with all new men, he was given a not-so-very-perfect Spad. The old-timers always got the new ones and the new men the old ones: that was a fortune of war. Hall's Spad was in flying condition, but its reconditioned engine was not very reliable.

Hall had been selected for the doubtful honor of making a patrol in honor of some visiting American brass hats. Bill Thaw would lead "the show," a term they had picked up from the British, and accompanying him would be Ted Parsons, Lufbery, William Dugan, Ray Bridgman and Jim Hall.

It would be Jim's third trip over the lines and he was warned by Bill to stay with the patrol. If he got lost he was to return to Chaudun and not go wandering about the sector, which was a tough one.

"We climb up to four thousand meters and rendezvous over the reservoir near Soissons," Bill had told them. "Then we'll form and go to patrol altitude." This meant they would rendezvous at 13,000 feet and then climb to 16,000 for their patrol. This was fine for the others, all old-timers with perfectly operating Hispano-Suiza engines. But Hall would have trouble getting up so high as fast as the others.

For a time it appeared he wouldn't even get off the ground. His tired old engine would not start. The poor *mécanos* tugged away at the prop, Jimmy flicked switches and toggles and nothing happened. Meanwhile the other five Spads took off. If ever Jimmy got started, they would meet him over the reservoir.

It was nearly fifteen minutes before the old engine wheezed to life. By this time Jimmy was pretty angry and disappointed. But getting aloft was only the first of his problems. He had to coax the Spad up to 13,000 feet—and by the time he got there the others had already left.

Albatros of the type used in the late months of the war.   G. B. Jarrett Collection

This was too much for Hall. He could have stayed within the French balloon lines and waited for the others to return, or he could have returned to Chaudun. Instead he turned his plane toward Rheims, hoping to catch sight of the five Spads. If he could keep the plane at the patrol altitude, Jim reasoned, he stood a good chance of catching up. His eyes narrowed as he studied the sector.

Just inside the German lines he saw a small formation. They were mere dots at this distance, but he could count them. Five planes! He pushed the throttle and dived for the formation. As he did he noted that there was another plane, just above the others, looping and rolling. That was Ray Bridgman enjoying himself, as he often did.

The only thing he did not understand was that there were six planes in that formation. He'd make seven. Oh, well, probably some stray had attached itself to Bill's patrol for safety.

Jimmy dived down and pulled himself up into the middle of the formation. Waggling his wings, he gave notice to the gang that he was ready for any action: bring on the dreaded foe! Feeling better after the earlier frustrations, Jim glanced around to see where the others were flying. Bill Thaw would of course be in the lead; that was Ray Bridgman up above. Where were the others?

A curious, not exactly describable feeling gripped Jim Hall in the area of the stomach.

He had flown right into the middle of a German patrol. Instead of six Spads, he was ringed in by six Albatros fighters. The action erupted in an instant. It did take a while for the German pilots to realize what had happened.

Those French pilots were becoming crazier every day. Now here was another, teasing them by dipping his wings and waving at them. There was no time for sporting fair play. They outnumbered him six to one—and there was a war on.

Jim Hall found an Albatros coming directly at him spitting fire. He jerked the rudder toward the French lines, hoping he could dive for home. The other Germans joined in as the lone Spad poised in the center of their fire.

Hall felt a rough slam in the shoulder as one slug struck him. Another sliced off his goggles and another plowed through his seat, creasing his groin. The bullet in his shoulder paralyzed his left arm, which now hung useless. Numbed with pain, Hall lost control of the Spad, which fell into a spin. One of the German planes followed its twisting path, pouring more Maxim slugs into the Spad.

With Hall drifting into unconsciousness, the Spad dived for the ground with full motor. Soon the speed made it impossible for the Germans to follow: besides, it was an obvious loss to the French. The Spad hurtled down to almost-certain destruction for 14,000 feet with Hall blacked out.

Momentarily Jim opened his eyes and realized foggily what was happening. He hauled back on the stick with his one good arm and the rugged Spad groaned, whined and otherwise complained, but pulled out of the death dive. Jim next switched off the engine; he didn't want to take the chance of burning. Then he fainted again as the Spad skimmed across the trenches of No Man's Land.

Jim had no idea whose trenches. He came to again and pulled the Spad out of another dive. He was barely 500 feet above the churned-up barb-wired earth. The Spad was flying directly in line with a trench as it came to earth with a smash. The fuselage fitted neatly into the trench as the wings snapped off, absorbing most of the shock of the crash. The plane gently settled to the bottom of the trench with the unconscious Jim Hall inside.

When Hall awakened he was on a stretcher being carried to a first-aid station. He wondered whether the stretcher-bearers were German or French. He groaned at the thought.

One of the others spoke, *"Tiens, petit! Ça va?* [Hello, little one! How goes it?]." Jimmy Hall's luck held. He had fallen inside the French lines, he had not been injured in the crash and the three wounds he had received were not serious. He was sent to a hospital to recover, after which he hoped to rejoin the Lafayette. The first time around he had lasted only ten days. He would be back. While recuperating from his wounds, James Hall kept himself busy by reading and also writing—a book about his own adventures. (Following the war he would become best known for *Mutiny on the Bounty* and other books written in collaboration with a friend from the Lafayette Flying Corps, Charles Nordhoff.)

Jim Hall was not the only man to leave the escadrille about this time. Fred Prince, Norman's brother, had left to become an instructor at Pau. Edward Hinkle had become ill and was released from military service. It had been Hinkle, working with Harold Willis, who had designed the final insignia of the Lafayette Escadrille. Laurence Rumsey, too, had become ill and was forced to leave the outfit.

Their empty places were quickly filled by new faces: Charles H. Dolan, Jr., of Boston, Henry S. Jones of Harford, Pennsylvania, Douglas MacMonagle from San Francisco, James R. Doolittle of New York (not the famed Jimmy Doolittle of the

Second World War); also from New York was Christopher W. Ford, the last American to join the Lafayette Escadrille. Louis Verdier-Fauvety came in to replace Arnoux de Maison-Rouge.

Doolittle was fated to serve with the escadrille for a very short time; the briefest, in fact, of all the members. He had joined them at the field at Chaudun in July 1917. He had already experienced bad luck while awaiting orders to go to the Front. He was flying at the replacement center one day when his plane lost speed and wing-slipped into the ground. After eight weeks in the hospital, Doolittle reported in at the escadrille. His face had been badly cut up but had healed nicely.

By this time Nivelle's offensive had gone sour and the squadron was to leave Chaudun to take part in the British campaign farther north. This would be the terrible attack in Flanders Fields. To be directly behind the Front the Lafayette men had to fly their Nieuports and Spads to the field at Saint-Pol-sur-Mer, just a mile and a half south of Dunkirk on the English Channel.

The day selected for the move, July 17, 1917, was not a good one. Ted Parsons described it as "greasy." The clouds lay thick, dark, close to the ground. It was hardly a day for a cross-

country flight of more than 200 miles. After taking off, the planes, separated in the clouds, broke up into little groups of two or three for the flight north. Ted Parsons had not bothered with a map, although he knew that Harold Willis had prepared one. Up in the clouds, Ted attached himself to Harold's tail and followed him north. From time to time they caught fleeting glimpses of the ground and were able to identify a village or river to orient themselves. Even with Harold's map, Ted Parsons had a suspicion that they were at least a little lost.

The two Spads came out over the English Channel and began searching along the coast for an airfield. Willis was in the lead and Parsons was not much more than twenty feet behind him. The mist and fog were swirling around them and blearing their goggles.

For no apparent reason, Harold Willis flipped over on one wing and banked sharply to one side. Without knowing why, Parsons did the same and shortly after "had a fleeting glimpse of a great gray bulk and two white faces in a wicker basket." Thanks to Willis' sharp vision, they had just missed colliding with the cable, nearly invisible in the thick clouds, of an English obser-

Chaudun, summer of 1917.   Courtesy Paul A. Rockwell

vation balloon. Had either plane struck the cable it would have meant a spectacular death for all, including the two men in the basket of the balloon.

Finally they were able to set down at Saint-Pol, where they were joined by the others. Only Doolittle, the newest replacement, had not arrived.

Like the others, Doolittle had become lost in the clouds. Before long he found himself all alone. He could see neither earth nor sky. He soon realized that he had to do something. Carefully he nosed his Spad down in a flat descent. At a couple of hundred feet he broke through the clouds and, by some miracle, found himself over an airdrome.

While he knew it couldn't be Saint-Pol-sur-Mer, at least he could drop down, check his fuel and get directions. He lined up with the runway, studying the field as he dropped lower and lower. Near the hangars there were a few planes lined up. He had flattened out for the landing when the machine guns opened up on him.

Doolittle could see the tracers spurting toward him and wondered what was going on. Instinctively he pushed the throttle ahead and yanked back on the stick. Out of the corner of his eye he caught a glimpse of a small group of men running around a plane, rolling it out and preparing it for takeoff. The plane had black crosses on the wings!

Doolittle had nearly landed on a German airfield.

Hastily he pulled away from the hornet's nest and sought refuge in the murky haven above. For the first time he was happy to be able to be alone. Anyway, he now knew the right way to Dunkirk, having ascertained his bearings over the German field.

He was even more certain when he momentarily came out into a clear patch of sky and saw a British observation balloon. But something was wrong. There were two German planes dodging in and out of the bloated clouds firing at the balloon. Trying to stand them off was a single British plane.

Doolittle gunned his Spad into a climb and rushed to the

Briton's aid. The German planes switched their attention from the balloon to the attacking planes. One swooped over and fastened himself onto Doolittle's tail and began firing. Almost with the first rounds Doolittle took a slug in the leg. The impact caused him to kick the Spad into a dive. The German stuck to him, though, and hammered away. Pieces of cowling were chipped away as a stream of lead struck the engine. Doolittle was now out of the fight.

The Spad skidded toward the earth as Doolittle fought to bring it under control. He had managed to straighten it out just before the wheels touched the earth. He had come into a plowed field at right angles to the furrows. The wheels stuck in a furrow and the Spad slammed over on its back. In the crash, Doolittle's face struck the rim of the cockpit and reopened the wounds from his previous accident.

British soldiers pulled him out of the plane and sent him to a hospital. After a slow recovery, James R. Doolittle was released from the French Air Service and returned to the United States. He had served fifteen days with the Lafayette Escadrille. Before he left he was awarded the *Croix de Guerre.*

The rest of the squadron waited at Saint-Pol-sur-Mer for something to do. They did find a fight or two, but it had not proved a very active sector. The big push in Flanders had bogged down in the mud and they were called upon to do very little. To while away the time they played cards, swam in the Channel, fished and honored their British colleagues with parties, in turn to be likewise honored. This cost a good deal of crockery and glasses, but it was good for releasing tension.

Bill Thaw had even found the fuselage of an abandoned Nieuport which he proceeded to transform into a boat. It was a comparatively lazy period.

It remained only for the inventive Ted Parsons to devise a unique form of diversion. In view of the fact that they were stationed just across the Channel from England Ted decided one sunny day that he might just pop over to London for "a bit of good old rare roast beef." There was, of course, a strict regulation against unauthorized Channel hops. Still, what harm could come from a friendly visit to an Ally?

On completing an uneventful morning patrol, Ted gassed up again and took off. He told no one his destination. Instead, he took off as usual and even flew along the coast a bit as he gained altitude before he "turned across the bright blue waters of the Channel."

What Ted did not know was that there was an order stating that every plane crossing the English Channel must be registered. The English on the other side were then to be informed of the departure time and the time it was to arrive. This was a normal precaution. The English had suffered a great deal from zeppelin airship raids, particularly during 1915–1916, and later from the big Gotha bombers. Smaller aircraft also might drop in and either strafe a city or drop bombs.

Winging his way, smacking his lips in anticipation of the rare roast beef, Ted Parsons sang a cheerful ditty or two. Good show, and all that and bless our English cousins!

In a few minutes he could see the famous white cliffs of Dover, and then "I got one of the jolliest receptions ever accorded a visiting airman from several straight-shooting English Archie batteries."

As an unregistered aircraft, Ted's Spad soon became the target for several batteries all along the coast. Angry puffs followed him along as he banked away from the white cliffs and turned back toward Dunkirk. No glory in being shot down by one's Allies. Besides, he had lost his appetite for beef.

Ted brought his Spad into the field and slunk off to his quarters. Very soon the repercussions came. As his was the only Spad up at that particular time, he was looked upon with no little suspicion by Captain Thénault. A full-scale investigation was launched to learn what had happened. Had some mad pilot flown over to England without authorization? Perish the thought! Or had a German intruder in a captured plane gone over for a visit? No matter, the Dover batteries had given him what for.

Luckily for Parsons he had been up too high for anyone to read the numbers on his Spad or to spot the whooping Indian on the side of the fuselage. When he was called into the Captain's office, Ted wore his most innocent expression and seemed horrified at the thought of the entire idea.

He was dismissed, though he noted a suspicious gleam in the Captain's eye. But the incident was closed and no disciplinary action was taken. Ted Parsons was content, like the others, to take advantage of the comparative quiet of their sector. It had proved a restful interval, a preparation for the next phase. The Flanders campaign was abandoned and Spa. 124 was ordered back to Verdun, to the field at Senard on the edge of the Argonne Forest.

What was up, the Americans wondered.

13 ACE OF ACES

The question was answered soon enough. After they had landed their Nieuports and Spads at Senard, they learned that once again they were to accompany about thirty Sopwith Strutters of Groupe de Bombardment 1 on an important bombing mission. There were hints of a new Big Push in the air. After the failure of his offensive, Nivelle's command was taken over by Marshal Henri Philippe Pétain, who moved rapidly to repair the damage done to the spirit of the suffering *poilu*. Besides improving conditions in the French Army, Pétain planned to launch a limited offensive. As a further boost to faltering morale, where else but at hallowed Verdun?

Instead of pouring men onto the battleground, Pétain decided to depend upon what was called "the weight of metal," a heavy field-artillery barrage. The celebrated French artillery would first prepare the field; only then would the *poilu* go over the top. Unlike so many carefully prepared plans, this one worked.

As further preparation, the bombers would visit Dun-sur-Meuse to strike at the large rail center there before the battle opened. This would close off, or at least seriously cripple, an important avenue of reinforcements and ammunition to the battlefield.

The Lafayette Escadrille had been sent to Senard to take part in this mission. Here they saw their first American soldiers—"doughboys" from an engineer battalion stationed nearby in the vicinity of the Argonne. It was through this tangled forest that the German line ran in this summer of 1917.

Before Pétain's push jumped off on August twentieth, the Strutters, with six Lafayette men providing cover, were detailed to bomb Dun-sur-Meuse on August eighteenth. It was a flight of about forty miles inside the lines—not very distant, but most of it over German-held territory. The raid would take place in daylight, promising a stiff fight going and coming.

Selected to accompany the Sopwith Strutters were Ted Parsons, Harold Willis, Walter Lovell, Stephen Bigelow, Henry Jones and Courtney Campbell. Campbell not many days before had survived his second flirting encounter with death when he crunched his wheels through the upper wing of Maison-Rouge's.

Because the bomber leader was in command of the mission, he decided how the fighters would be used. He split the Americans into two groups of three which were ordered to remain on either side of the bomber formation. It accomplished little for Captain Thénault to point out that if the Spads were tied down to such positions it would be impossible for them to maneuver and to protect the Strutters properly.

This meant also that the faster Spads would have to zigzag throughout the mission in order to stay with the slow Sopwiths. Ted Parsons cursed his lot as he traced aimless S patterns alongside the lumbering bombers. The Archie had given them a hot reception as they flew toward Dun-sur-Meuse. He was flying on the left flank of the bombers. Nearby he could see Harold Willis doing the same thing.

They passed over the Argonne and were into the German lines when out of the sun flashed three German Albatroses. As Hank Jones phrased it, "they filtered right straight down and went through the whole thing." On the sides, where they had been ordered to stay, the men in the Spads saw the Germans shooting up the Sopwiths.

It was impossible, of course, to cut through the formation to fight off the Albatroses. Glued to the formation's flanks because they were ordered to fly there, they could not gain altitude and intercept the German fighters.

Very quickly the sky was infested with multicolored German fighter planes and scribbled over with smoke and the thin lines of tracer bullets. Ted Parsons suddenly detected some black specks to his left, and tracers soon ripped through his wings. Three Albatroses converged on Ted, and for him the high cold air grew suddenly hot.

Harold Willis was about seventy yards to Ted's left and above him when the attack came. Seeing his friend in trouble, Harold dived in firing. He discouraged the Albatros on Ted's tail. But then he found himself in plenty of trouble. There was a snarling Albatros on his tail. By this time it was every man for himself, for the German fighters had swarmed out in great numbers.

Hoping to elude his pursuer, Willis pulled up into an Immelmann turn (a climbing turn which sometimes confused the pursuer who continued to climb after his adversary had already switched directions). That was little help, for more German fighters jumped in, machine guns flashing. Willis jockeyed the Spad all over the sky in a vain attempt to keep out of the line of fire, but early in the fight his engine received a number of hits. It sputtered and groaned, missed and started as Harold tried to fend off his attackers, fight and keep his Spad in the air, all at the same time.

As he lost altitude, the men in the Albatroses raked him with crossfire from every angle. More slugs struck the engine, brace wires split and curled away uselessly, struts chipped and fabric peeled into the slipstream. The tracers hissed by uncomfortably close as Harold's windshield disappeared. Then, with a smack, his goggles were torn away. Though he was not struck himself, the bullet hitting his goggles stunned Harold for a moment.

The fight had worked its way close to the ground from 12,000 feet. Harold knew he would have to land or be chopped to bits by the Albatroses. He picked out a hill not far from Dun-sur-Meuse and brought his Spad down. The Albatros pilot landed nearby and took charge to keep his victim out of the hands of the German infantry, who were not very gentle with aviators.

Harold Willis on that day became the first—and, it turned out, only—American to be taken prisoner while serving with the Lafayette Escadrille. He made a curious impression upon his gentlemanly hosts when he was taken to their mess and treated to coffee and lunch. He shocked the very proper Germans with his uniform. Harold Willis had taken off on the Dun-sur-Meuse mission wearing only a pair of loud green striped pajamas and an old brown sweater under his flying suit. The Americans were apparently an odd bunch. After the ceremony of being honored by his foes, Harold Willis was driven off to a prison. In time he managed to escape and worked his way into Switzerland.

Before all this happened, the battle over Dun-sur-Meuse had become one confusing dogfight with twisting and turning planes shooting at one another. The Strutters had bombed the target and winged around in a great circle to head for home. The men in the Spads had their hands full, for they were greatly outnumbered by the German fighters.

There was little order to the battle now. Planes dived this way and that, firing their guns. One of the Strutters burst into flame and made its final plunge. Walter Lovell spotted another hemmed in by several Albatroses and dived in. He shot one away from the tail of the French plane. Seeing their companion burning, the other Germans fled, leaving the struggling Strutter to totter back to Senard.

As they came closer to the lines the attacks became less ferocious, but not before Stephen Bigelow dived to the defense of a Strutter suffering under the attack of six Albatroses. Though he drove them off, Bigelow received a bad face wound when struck by a bullet which tore away his windshield. Despite the loss of blood, Bigelow brought the Spad back to the field. He was later cited for his defense of the French bomber and, because of his wound, released from the service.

Except for Harold Willis, an unhappy guest of the Kaiser, all the others fought their way back to Senard. It had been a hard-fought mission. Two bombers of thirty-one were lost, and one Spad. Though possibly other Germans were knocked down, only Walter Lovell's kill was confirmed as official.

But, thanks to Courtney Campbell, the day's thrills were not yet complete. Because of the long, narrow layout of the field at Senard and the large number of planes using the field, certain strict traffic regulations were in force. All landing planes were supposed to taxi all the way to the end of the runway, turn and then taxi to their own hangars. No one was supposed to land and then turn into his hangar, even if he was directly opposite it.

And no one did—except Campbell.

Just as his Spad touched down, Campbell noted that the path to the side was clear. He jammed the rudder and turned the nose of his plane toward the Lafayette hangars instead of continuing on down to the end of the field. At the same instant one of the Sopwith Strutters was settling down for its landing.

The pilot saw the Spad directly in his path but realized that with his power down he would not be able to yank the bomber back into the air. He closed his eyes.

The Sopwith struck directly on top of Campbell's plane. There was a resounding *Crunch!* The Spad squashed down to the ground, its landing gear snapped; a wheel went bouncing along the runway and bits of fabric and wing ribs scattered about as the propeller of the bomber chewed away at the wing.

The Sopwith miraculously regained its balance and managed to land safely, if crazily. The Spad, however, rolled end over end under the impact of the collision, ripping and crunching and generally disintegrating as it went along.

The meat wagon raced out to the spot where the Spad lay now in the form of a tattered ball. A number of men ran out to extricate Campbell from the wreck. When the first of them arrived at the dusty pile, there stood Campbell, hardly the worse for wear. He was a little rumpled, but his composure was untouched. As the astounded men watched, he took out a crumpled pack of cigarettes, placed a slightly bent one in his mouth, lighted it and walked away. He had cheated sure death the third time. For some reason, he once more got off with little more than a scolding from the Captain for a serious breach of discipline.

He would yet learn that he could charm his way out of punishment, but death continued to wait for him. And with death, charm was no argument.

Ted Parsons was to recall that "based at the flying field of Senard, we went in for some really intensive air work, the most exhausting of all our campaigns." Not only had they moved to a most active front, they arrived there in time for a most unusual spell of good weather.

For more than three solid weeks every day dawned bright and clear—"twenty-four successive days of brilliant sunshine, a great rarity in France," Parsons wrote, "and the total flying hours piled up in that one month alone was staggering." Most of the Americans flew at least three patrols a day. There was no shortage of Germans and opportunity for combat.

After one fierce encounter Kenneth Marr nursed his Spad home even though all the control wires to his elevators (wires that controlled the up-and-down movement of the plane) had been shot off. By changing the speed of the engine he managed to keep the elevators in line by the speed of the air rushing around them. When he wanted to drop the nose of the plane he simply slowed the engine. Thus jockeying the plane, he returned safely to Senard, using the engine instead of his conventional controls.

Ted Parsons, after what must have been dozens of fights and victories, scored his first official victory in a typical adventure. On the morning of September 4, 1917, he took off in the company of Dudley Hill and Robert Rockwell for a little tour over the Meuse. Both Hill and Rockwell were forced by engine trouble to return to Senard. Waving them off, Ted proceeded with the patrol, keeping inside the French lines at around 15,000 feet.

On their side of the lines he warily watched a large formation of German Albatroses, possibly ten. They too kept to their side of the Meuse. As he flew along, his engine purring beautifully, Ted kept an eye on the German formation below as well as some French observation planes moving slowly along. He was certain that the Germans saw both the French reconnaissance planes and his lone Spad.

One of the French planes was a big two-engine ship carrying three passengers. For a few minutes it strayed away from the formation. Two Albatroses streaked across the line for the attack, no doubt hoping to get in some bursts before running back into their own lines.

Ted Parsons had his own ideas. He had the advantage of altitude, and his Spad could outdive and outrun an Albatros. He nosed down too. With engine full out, the Spad dropped upon the attacking German planes. Kicking his feet back and forth, which moved the bullet streams from side to side, Ted sprayed the two intruders as he dived.

The Albatroses fanned away as Ted streaked by. He passed the French plane also. Not wanting the Germans to get the advantage, Ted pulled the Spad up in a steep climb. Out of nowhere loomed a German observation plane he had not seen until that instant. It was a certain collision, Ted feared. He violently pulled the Spad away as the German two-seater grew larger and larger in his sights. As he careened off, Ted squeezed the trigger of his Vickers.

The monstrous German plane staggered in midair as Ted fell off into a spin. By the time he recovered from the spin he saw the plane wallowing and drifting downward. Then the nose dropped and it dived for the ground, leaving the top wing behind and trailing pieces of fuselage. At last an official! It was the first of eight enemy planes that Ted Parsons would shoot down.

Not many battles ended so happily, of course. Late in September Lufbery led a patrol over the lines. Following him were Charles Dolan, "Doc" Rockwell and Douglas MacMonagle. For Douglas it was to be a very special day: somehow his mother had traveled all the way from San Francisco to the battle zone. Even more mysteriously, she had been granted permission to visit her son right behind the lines. Doug was scheduled to pick her up at the little railroad station at Ravenel after he returned from the patrol.

As they flew along sharp-eyed Luf spotted a number of Albatroses hiding in the sun. His plan was to turn toward the French lines, get the advantage of altitude and drop down on the Germans. He waggled his wings and was followed by Rockwell and Dolan.

But where was Doug?

When next Luf saw him he was plunging directly at the Albatros formation; it was too late for the others to go to his aid. Everything was over in seconds. MacMonagle plowed into the formation, and then his Spad went straight down into the woods near Triaucourt, inside the French lines.

MacMonagle's mother finally arrived at Ravenel tragically in time for her son's funeral.

A week later Courtney Campbell and Hank Jones were on patrol over the lines, where they attacked four German two-seaters circling about directing artillery fire. Leading the attack, Jones dived under the Hanoveraners, hoping to pull under their unprotected bellies.

He was terribly surprised to discover that the Germans had devised a system whereby a gun could be fired through the bottom of the plane. He ran into a shattering hail of bullets. The battle was decided in that instant. His Spad was profusely punctured; the fuel tank leaked and several bracing wires trailed loosely in the wind. Hank Jones realized he had to head for home. As he dived for the comparative safety of the French lines, he looked back but couldn't see Courtney Campbell anywhere.

There wasn't another plane visible in the sky.

Campbell, true to his temperament, was at the moment in headlong pursuit of the two-seaters across and beyond the German lines. He was so intent on the chase that he either didn't notice how deeply he was going into German-held territory or he didn't care. It was a foolish but typical gesture.

Death, which he had tempted so often before, waited for Campbell. He ran directly into a German fighter which had been assigned to protect the two-seaters. Campbell streaked directly at the Albatros with his Vickers sputtering. The twin Spandaus above the nose of the Albatros twinkled and as smoke curled away from the muzzles Campbell's Spad tottered for a fraction of a moment, then lurched into a spin.

His plane crashed heavily inside the German lines. Because a few days later the spot was taken by the French in an infantry attack there was no word of Campbell's fate: as far as the squadron was concerned, he had simply disappeared. It was a full month before the pilot who had shot Campbell down was able to drop a message behind the lines. Attached to the message was a memorial wreath.

Only Bill Thaw and Raoul Lufbery, with the Captain, the longest-surviving members of the escadrille, seemed to have the kind of luck that Campbell had had until it ran out. Bill Thaw, as a lieutenant, was still the only commissioned American in the

Major Raoul Lufbery, U. S. Aero Service, 1918.   U. S. Signal Corps Photo: National Archive

French Army. Luf was by then an adjutant, a rank somewhere between sergeant and second lieutenant.

The quiet yet smoldering Luf was the escadrille's star, its Ace of Aces. His every move was reported in the French and American newspapers. He was decorated regularly and cited time after time in the dispatches from Army headquarters. Luf was a celebrity, even to the point of having babies named for him and receiving fan letters from lovesick girls.

Luf took this adulation, though he could not quite understand it, in his stride. He remained a simple though mysterious figure. He did not reveal himself to any man in the squadron, did not discuss his "future" plans with anyone, did not have a favorite buddy. He had seen too many of his friends go west. Though he was liked, even admired by his squadron mates and was in turn obviously fond of them, his best friends were Whiskey and Soda, the lion cubs who now had grown quite large.

Throughout his service with the Lafayette Escadrille, even after he had become its major attraction, Luf never changed. He was a good although distant friend and he could always be depended upon in a fight. Unaffected by the hero worship, Luf went about his grim business.

As on the ground, Luf in the air was primarily a loner. After he completed his daily patrols with the squadron, during which he performed magnificently as a member of a team, Luf liked to go out on his own to hunt. In a free-for-all Luf could be counted upon to keep an Albatros off a patrolmate's tail. He would be all over the sky, keeping the Germans away from a green pilot out for his first combat flight. If on the ground Luf preferred to keep his distance, in the air he tended his brood with a mother's love.

On a lone patrol Luf exercised no love. He was cunning; he took full advantage of all the tricks. He swooped down out of the sun, he used clouds as old American frontiersmen had used trees to hide behind. He knew how to use the strength, diving power and speed of his Spad to take the enemy by surprise, streak through his formation and hit and run.

To Luf, air fighting was not sport. The only sporting aspect of his long series of "kills" was that most of them (the official ones, that is, which numbered fewer than half of his actual victories) were two-seaters. This meant that Luf, with his single gun, fought against odds even though he had perfected his flying, shooting and tactics to a remarkable degree.

By September 4, 1917, when the squadron was stationed at Senard for the Dun-sur-Meuse raid, Lufbery had accounted for eleven official planes shot down. These did not include the dozen or more he had destroyed far behind the lines either on lone-eagle patrols or in formation. His final score, when the war ended the following year, was seventeen. For a long period after America came into the war Luf was the American Ace of Aces, as well as the Lafayette's Ace.

In 1917 Luf was past thirty. But except for his rheumatism, he was a perfect physical specimen. His reflexes were quick, his coordination perfect and he had the vision of an eagle (unlike some in the squadron, who were nearly half-blind). Of course, there was a tremendous strain on the body in the early days of air combat, before the days of oxygen masks and electrically heated flying suits.

But with his superb eyesight and tough, chunky body, Luf stood up very well. He seemed constructed of square blocks of concrete: short and compact with a squarish head set on a powerful neck. He was the prototype of what, in a later more terrible air war, would be the perfect fighter pilot.

Just why he loved to hunt alone Lufbery never explained. By 1917 the era of the lone eagles was really over. Air leaders had learned the importance of flying in formation. It may have been that, because he was so conscientious a patrol leader, Luf did not wish to place anyone else's life in jeopardy. He did not seem terribly interested in being the Ace of Aces. But he was almost always out, combing the skies: the deadly hunter. He did not kill for pleasure; he often spoke with pity for "the poor devils" he had knocked down.

Nor was Luf completely invincible. He would return from patrols with his plane in tatters and other signs of a near-visit from the Grim Reaper. Luf laughed when he counted the bullet holes. Following one fight in which he and Ted Parsons had tangled with a half-dozen German planes, Luf returned with forty different punctures in his plane.

He laughed, but he did not reveal his fears, if he had any. Once he is supposed to have said, in a rare moment, "There won't be any after-the-war for the fighter pilot."

14 END OF THE GREAT ADVENTURE

Early in December 1917 word filtered down that all of the Americans who wished to transfer from the Lafayette Escadrille into the United States Air Service could do so by requesting a release from the French.

Dr. Gros, who had been so important to the initial formation of the escadrille, was busy again. He accepted a commission as major in the United States Air Service. Ambitious for the future of his Lafayette Flying Corps, of which the Lafayette Escadrille was a part, Major Gros traveled all along the Front from Verdun to the North Sea. With him went a small group of other American officers who examined and interviewed almost every American serving with the French.

All of the Lafayette men except Ted Parsons, who was home on leave at the time, applied for transfer to the U.S. Air Service. There were some delays. The French were understandably not eager to release so many men at one time. It would have left several of their combat squadrons short-handed. The French, as

On the move: the Lafayette Escadrille disbands and its members are sent to American squadrons forming in France, April 1918.

U. S. Air Force Photo

they proved when Norman Prince first began his formation of the American squadron, were expert at creating confusion on paper—in triplicate.

Worse, they were outdone by the Americans at their own game. The sleeping giant, America, had awakened to the nightmare of war. But it was not yet ready. There were delays, mixups, arguments and general ill will. To make it still worse, there was a shake-up in the command of the American Air Service just about the time the transfers were to take place. This not only delayed the changeover, it began the process all over again.

The Americans were released by the French around Christmas 1917. But they were not yet accepted by the Americans. They had been cut adrift with no place to go. Thus did the men of the Lafayette Escadrille chalk up another "First" to their credit. For almost two months they fought in a world war as civilians. Although technically released by the French, they decided to remain at the Front until the U.S.A.S. made up its mind.

When all the paperwork had begun the escadrille was moved from Chaudun to La Noblette in the Champagne sector. The Allies were preparing for the expected big German spring offensive. There was little flying out of La Noblette—which because of its discomforts reminded the men of the horrible field at Cachy. Often the airfield lay deep in snow and they had little to do but crouch around the almost worthless stoves, shivering and griping about the inefficiency of the high command of the American Air Service.

There were further complications. When the new regime, led by nonairman General Benjamin Foulois, took over, it brought with it any number of new rules and ideas. The U.S. Air Service was a youthful outfit and willing enough to substitute energy for experience. Its organization too often engaged in its own private war; petty jealousies led to disagreements, pointless hairsplitting and curious decisions.

For example, according to the new rules almost every member of the Lafayette Escadrille, fourteen at this time, was unfit to fly.

This was news, indeed! Several, including Lufbery, Soubiran and Marr, were over thirty. Others—Thaw, Hill and Dolan—would never be aviators because of poor vision! This decision was made despite the fact that Thaw had been flying since before the war, Hill had flown for three years and Dolan for fourteen months.

It took a special waiver from General John J. Pershing himself to make aviators of many of the Lafayette Escadrille men. He pointed out in his telegram to Washington that the experience of these "old" and "physically disabled" men would be valuable for building an American air force in France.

In the same telegram Pershing also recommended that the men be given commissions in the U.S. Army. All, except Bill Thaw, who was a lieutenant, and Raoul Lufbery, a *Sous-Lieutenant*, were enlisted men. Pershing believed they should be given ranks equal to their experience, around which the Air Service could then build.

Clearly the intention was to form a squadron around Bill Thaw and Luf, who were commissioned majors. The only problem was that when he reported into Issoudun, the big American aviation center, Luf had no squadron to command. The 95th Aero Squadron existed only on paper. Major Raoul Lufbery, man of action and superb teacher, was buried for many miserable weeks at Issoudun sharpening pencils, his feet on his desk, making salty remarks about the U.S. Air Service.

Around this same confused time James Norman Hall, after a stay in the hospital, was assigned by mistake to Escadrille Spa. 112. His luck still held, for things continued to happen to him. He nearly got himself court-martialed for his attempts to return to the Lafayette. Finally, however, Captain Thénault managed to get the French red tape unsnarled and Hall once again flew the Spads with the whooping-Indian sign.

He began the new year—1918—in grand style. With Bill Thaw he went out on New Year's Day for a look over the lines. In the clouds, their two Spads became separated; each went his own way. Hall flew around for a while searching for Bill and enjoying the snow-covered vista below him. He forgot for some moments that he was out on a patrol until he spotted a distant speck and, deciding it was Bill, flew over to join him.

When he came closer Jim discovered he had blundered upon a lone Albatros. The German was obviously unaware of his approach. Using Luf's technique of sneaking up on his victim, Hall came in closer. He did not like to strike in that fashion; it somehow disturbed his sense of fair play. Still he recalled the death of Doug MacMonagle on the day of his mother's visit—and of some of the others. And the war. . . .

Now the Albatros was centered in the sight. Jimmy pulled the trigger. He was so close by this time that he could watch the slugs striking the fuselage, battering into the engine and flicking away bits of wood and metal.

The Albatros turned, dropped its nose and fell. Jimmy lost sight of it in the clouds, but the crash was witnessed by some French soldiers in the trenches. On his return he was met by Bill, who had already returned, and the new French second-in-command Louis Verdier-Fauvety, who scolded Jim for losing Thaw on the patrol. But when the Albatros was confirmed all was forgiven.

It was a historic confirmation; it was Jim Hall's first, and the last victory credited to the Lafayette Escadrille.

The early months of 1918 were generally poor for flying. There were routine patrols when the weather permitted, but very little action. The Germans were saving their planes for the Big Push, which came in the spring with a series of five different offensives. Once again the Germans saw the tip of the Eiffel Tower, and such names as the Marne and the Somme stood for fierce battles, as they had in 1914–1916.

There was a stunning breakthrough as the Germans gambled desperately. The Germans hoped that they might drive the British and French to their knees before the Americans were ready for real combat. It had almost worked, but the stubborn British held, and so did the gallant French. The few American troops already in France helped hold the line. The giants who laughed a lot, boasted almost as much, proved themselves in battle. To the exhausted British and French their untried freshness meant the difference between surrender and continuing with the war.

By the late summer the Allies, under command of Field Marshal Ferdinand Foch, struck with a jarring counteroffensive. The green Americans distinguished themselves in the fighting at Saint-Mihiel, in the Argonne Forest and in the aerial fighting over the battlefields.

By this time, Raoul Lufbery had been released from his desk at Issoudun and given command of the 94th Aero Squadron. In time, his original 95th too would emerge as a real fighting unit. The 94th, which became famed as the "Hat-in-Ring" squadron, would produce under Luf's teaching such fine airmen as Douglas Campbell, Reed Chambers and Edward Rickenbacker—who, by the end of the war, would be America's top-scoring flyer.

There were still hitches. Although the 94th was equipped with the new Nieuport 28s, the guns had not yet arrived. All Luf could do was take his fledglings out for practice patrols safely away from the lines. The guns arrived in April 1918, one year after the American declaration of war.

It seemed that Luf spent most of the early weeks of the 94th's existence growling. He was cheered up when Jimmy Hall appeared—he was a welcome reminder of the simpler days with the Lafayette. Jimmy was able to add two more "officials" to his score before he experienced his final aerial escapade.

On May seventh he took off on a patrol which included Rickenbacker. They were flying the new Nieuport 28s. This beautifully proportioned plane had been used for a while by the Lafayette but was taken out of service because of an unfortunate tendency. In a prolonged, steep dive the fabric of the upper wing peeled off. The Americans were issued these planes only because there were no others readily available.

On this fateful patrol Hall dived on an Albatros and soon

found himself the victim of the Nieuport's defect. He was concentrating on the German plane and heard an unexpected *Crack!* Looking in the direction of the sound, he saw that the fabric had ripped back on the top wing and the tatters flapped wildly in the wind. Jimmy forgot about the Albatros. He carefully guided the Nieuport out of its dive and steered for home.

His day, however, was not over. There was one other problem. In passing over the German Archie positions near the lines he was brought under severe antiaircraft fire. It was uncomfortable, but to a veteran like Jim, no great worry. Archie rarely hit anything.

There was a sudden lurch, the engine ripped and heaved, then stopped. Mystified, Hall wondered what else could have gone wrong. There was no mystery about his future: he knew that the war was over for James Hall. He would have to land behind the enemy lines. There was nothing further to do except nurse the battered plane down for as gentle a landing as possible.

Though he was slightly battered by the landing, Jimmy was able to examine the plane. An Archie shell had scored a direct hit on his engine but had failed to explode. The impact had knocked the engine loose and the shell remained imbedded in it, without exploding, all the way down. Hall's luck had held out to the end. He spent the remaining six months of the war in a German prison camp.

Luf was quite upset by the loss of Jim Hall. He scowled and raged, but to no avail. He swore vengeance but he had no luck—no new victories to add to his score of seventeen. He continued his practice of going out alone, as he had with the Lafayette, but no Germans emerged to become Luf's victims. There seemed to be a great shortage of German planes in the sector.

Then on Sunday morning, May 19, 1918, the impossible happened. A lone Albatros two-seater ventured over the lines on a photographic mission. Its progress was marked by white antiaircraft bursts until it wavered almost directly over the field at Toul, where the 94th was based.

There was a good deal of excitement and flurry as men rushed to their planes. Engines roared and men shouted until finally one Nieuport, piloted by young, inexperienced Oscar Gude, Jr., rose to challenge the intruder.

Luf watched with rising anger as Gude emptied his guns at too great a range and never even nicked the Albatros. Luf ran to a hangar where another Nieuport was getting ready to take off. In its cockpit sat another green pilot.

Luf dashed to the quivering plane and shouted, "Out!"

The pilot scrambled out and Luf jumped into the cockpit. He pushed the throttle and the Nieuport roared across the field and with the rotary engine snarling rose straight into the sky. With the advantage of his faster plane, Luf quickly overtook the Albatros, which seemed to hover lazily near the field. The men on the ground relaxed as they gathered to watch the famous Raoul Lufbery, American Ace of Aces, perform.

Luf climbed to a position behind and above the Albatros and then dived, firing his twin Vickers guns as he raced in. For seconds it appeared to the men watching that he would collide with the Albatros. But then he swerved and pulled away. For some reason, perhaps because his guns had jammed, Luf spent some time circling.

The trouble cleared, he dived again upon the Albatros. As Lufbery bore down on the sluggish German plane the Nieuport suddenly went ablaze. It passed right by the German plane trailing great sheets of flame.

As the horrified men on the ground watched they saw Lufbery fall free of the flaming Nieuport and plummet a mile through empty air. It would never be known whether he had fallen or had preferred a swift death rather than a slow burning agony. His only wound from the fight with the Albatros was a bullet through his left hand.

Luf fell into the garden of a village shoemaker. By the time his friends arrived, Luf's shattered body had been covered with flowers from nearby French gardens.

Where Lufbery fell after leaving his burning plane.

This simple, heartfelt tribute to Luf was a fitting monument to him and to those who had gone before: Douglas MacMonagle, Courtney Campbell, Edmond Genêt, Ronald Hoskier, James McConnell, Norman Prince, Kiffin Rockwell, Victor Chapman. To the dead, and to the living as well, it was the most eloquent memorial of all because it was so honestly simple.

Luf's death left only Bill Thaw of the original few. Only he was fated of those who had begun at Luxeuil to serve through the war. By its close he was a lieutenant colonel and commanded an entire group, the 3rd Pursuit. It was made up of the 28th, 93rd, 103rd and 213th squadrons. All used some variation of an Indianhead for their individual squadron insignias.

Captain Thénault had meanwhile been assigned to the school of acrobatics at Pau as Chief Pilot.

Ted Parsons returned from his leave, cast a critical eye upon the flounderings of the U.S. Air Service and elected to remain in the French Air Service. He even hoped to form another Lafayette Escadrille, but was soon discouraged in that by both the French and the Americans. He was welcomed into the Escadrille Spa. 3, one of the legendary *Cigognes* squadrons. This was the escadrille in which the French folk hero Georges Guynemer had served until the day he took off and never returned. Because no trace was found of him for some time (his plane and body were obliterated in an artillery barrage), French schoolchildren and many adults came to believe that Guynemer, the immortal, had flown "so high that he could not come down."

Thus did Ted Parsons acquire a unique distinction: he was the only American to serve in the two most celebrated French escadrilles of the First World War. While flying with the Storks, Ted Parsons accounted for seven official victories, ending the war with a total of eight.

The others served with distinction also. Robert Rockwell took over command of the 103rd Aero Squadron after Bill Thaw; when Rockwell left to command another squadron his replacement was Robert Soubiran. Dudley Hill commanded the 138th Aero Squadron until given even greater responsibilities as commander of the 5th Pursuit Group. Ray Bridgman commanded the 22nd Squadron, Kenneth Marr the 94th (before Ricken-

The 103rd Squadron, ex-Lafayette Escadrille, assembles at the Front. In charge

backer took over) and David Peterson the 95th. Charles Dolan and Henry Jones, the youngsters, did extraordinarily well as flight commanders in the 103rd ("Lafayette") Aero Squadron. William Dugan was transferred from the 103rd to Orly as Officer in Charge of Repair and Testing at the American Acceptance Park.

Pershing had been right: an effective air force could be formed around such men.

Christopher Ford, a New Yorker and the last man to join the Lafayette Escadrille, had come to it directly from flight school. Through some error in his orders he had never attended the schools of acrobatics and gunnery before being shipped to the Front. He should not have lasted more than a few days. Instead, with the help of the others and by virtue of his own courage, he survived. He learned the very necessary skills the hard way: in actual combat.

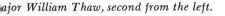
ajor William Thaw, second from the left.   U. S. Signal Corps Photo: National Archives

Serving with the 103rd Squadron after the changeover, Chris Ford emerged as a fine flight leader and accounted for two official victories in a series of scorching aerial battles. The two planes Ford shot down were the latest Fokker D–7s, probably the finest fighter plane developed during the war.

Then on October 15, 1918, Ford's Spad was struck by ground fire as he led a patrol over the German lines. Forced to land in enemy territory, he was soon on his way to a prison camp at Villingen.

The Great War finally churned itself out within a month. On November 11, 1918, the Armistice was signed and the slaughter and waste came to an end. With an almost shocking suddenness the guns were silent. After almost four years peace was more unreal than war.

At Villingen the Germans, confused, demoralized, stunned, simply did not know what to do. Some slipped away, others fell into an inertia as if waiting for someone to tell them what the next move should be. Tired of waiting for his release, Chris Ford acted with characteristic Lafayette spirit. He and several other prisoners just walked out of the prison and started for the lines.

In a couple of days they had covered a distance of about sixty miles. Just as they walked from the east into the city of Colmar, French soldiers were entering from the west.

Colmar was situated a little to the west of the Rhine River in the foothills of the Vosges Mountains. It was only about an hour's flying time—in a *Bébé* Nieuport—from Luxeuil, where on a spring morning in 1916 the young eagles had first spread their wings.

But now, so many painful months later, winter had come to France as Chris Ford, weary and cold, trudged into Colmar. Winter had come—and peace—to a ravaged land.

The great adventure was finished.

okker D-VII, *produced in the last months of the war and one of the finest fighter planes* the 1914-1918 *conflict. Had it appeared sooner, it would have taken a terrible toll of* e *Allied airmen.*

U. S. Air Force Photo